Veloce Publishing Presents

A **Paul Veysey** Production

MOTOR MOVIES
- The Posters!

VELOCE PUBLISHING
THE PUBLISHER OF FINE AUTOMOTIVE BOOKS

Other great Veloce books –

WWW.VELOCE.CO.UK

First published in August 2007 by Veloce Publishing Limited, 33 Trinity Street, Dorchester DT1 1TT, England. Fax 01305 268864/e-mail info@veloce.co.uk/web www.veloce.co.uk or www.velocebooks.com.
ISBN: 978-1-845841-27-0/UPC: 6-36847-04127-4

INTRODUCTION

Motor Movies – The Posters is not intended to be a comprehensive reference work for every movie poster that has ever contained a set of wheels. That way would lie madness for me, and boredom for you. Besides, there are hundreds of other fact-filled works in which you can check for my mistakes.

Some things are irrefutable: there will be times when no amount of research will reveal the name of a poster artist, there are occasions where the identity of a vehicle is lost, or has become highly debatable in the 'artists's impression'. Equally, I have not attempted to make the posters look perfect; certainly, some have been preserved and linen-backed, but most are in 'cinema-used' condition, with that patina of age and handling that can make the poster even more beautiful.

What *Motor Movies* is designed to do is place before the reader the beautiful, the fascinating, and the bizarre ways in which the motor car (and occasionally its 'siblings' (bikes, boats, commercial vehicles, etc) has been depicted since the early days of cinema. We will not be detailing plot lines, the lives of the stars, or too much of the minutiae of the – sometimes graphically over-ambitious – vehicles that appear here.

The movies featured in the book haven't been chosen for their social relevance, cult status, or box office takings. Mostly, the movies haven't been chosen at all; this is about the publicity for those movies, the artistry and inventiveness of the posters and lobby cards.

You'll find a rarity rating for each poster, and, when arcane detail is available, you shall have it. You'll note that many of the posters have fold lines, and, in some cases, fold separations. This is because, prior to the early 1980s, almost all posters were machine-folded post-printing, before being dispatched to the distributor and various cinemas. These folds have worn over the years of being displayed in cinemas – and thereafter – collections. Later 'glossy paper' posters made folding impractical, as the image would often crack when folded. It's only relatively recently in poster history that they've been rolled instead.

And, of course, none of these posters should be available to us at all as, after being displayed in the cinema, they should have been returned to their respective distributor for pulping.

In the glossary you will find a rough guide to some of the jargon associated with movie posters, and a note of the sizes in which many countries produced their posters. For the most part, these sizes are a pretty good guide when considering the originality of a poster. Another guide is paper quality: if it's too good, especially pre-1970s, watch out!

While original movie posters have become fine investments, the golden rule is: buy the posters you really like, then your enjoyment is guaranteed and any profit is a bonus.

The 'rarity rating' I've used is purely personal, and goes like this:

1 You can go to your local poster shop and get one
2 I can get another
3 I can possibly get another
4 The chances of my getting another are very remote
5 If I ever get another, you can shave my legs and call me Mimsy

Enjoy *Motor Movies – The Posters*, and feel free to email me (paul@drivepast.com) if you want to know more, or feel I need to know more.

ACKNOWLEDGEMENTS & THANKS

Firstly to Helen, for her patience, her love – and for driving me home from the pub.

To Matt Simpson, for accepting that I'm a technological nitwit, and holding my hand; for the technical creation and servicing of the Drivepast website, and more particularly for taking on the task of photography for this book.

To Simon Tyrrell, for Dolores, the map reading, and the Speed Crazed pic.

To Mick Walsh of *Classic and Sports Car* for planting the seed.

To Mark Dixon of *Octane*, for the Drivepast photoshoot.

To Roger and Ben, gentleman racers, for access to Fangio.

To Francois for the reference library, and the unfailing ability to buy a great supper.

To the studios, and the artists and designers – nonymous and anonymous – who supplied the material for this book; my grateful thanks.

Many of the movies mentioned in this book are available on DVD and cassette. Hunt them down: the good ones are nearly as entertaining as the bad ones ...

Paul Veysey
Tibberton, Gloucestershire
www.drivepast.com
paul@drivepast.com
0044 (0)1452 790672

THE LIGHTS OF LONDON

Movie made in the UK in 1914 • Lobby card: USA • Size: 11x14in (28x36cm) • Rarity rating: 5
Motor: Unknown • Players: Arthur Chesney

Arthur Chesney starred in this mostly forgotten movie. This US lobby card has been hand-coloured

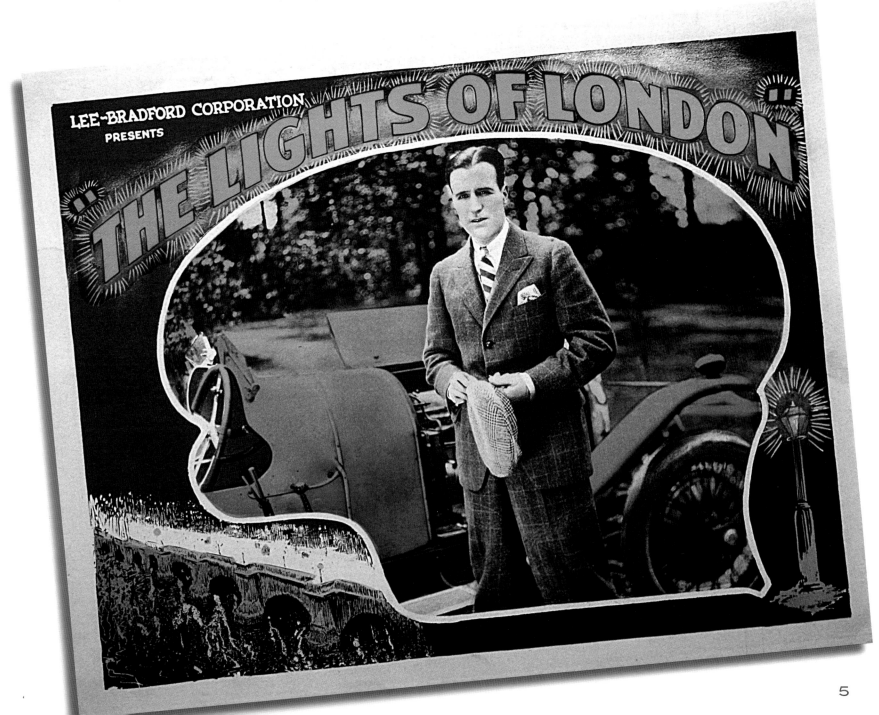

EL AUTOMOVIL GRIS

Movie made in Mexico in 1919 • Lobby card: Mexico • Size: 17x13in (43x33cm) • Rarity rating: 4
Motor: Studebaker • Players: Joaquin Coss, Dora Vila

A story of crime and vengeance south of the border. Known north of the border as *The Grey Automobile*

SPEED CRAZED

Movie made in the USA in 1926
Poster: Belgium
Size: 24x33in (61x 84cm)
Rarity rating: 5
Motor: Early racers; artist's impression
Players: Billy Sullivan

One of the finest pieces of motor racing art in any area. The title *Speed Crazed* was changed to the more prosaic *180 a l'Heure* (with reference to 180kph) for the Belgian market

THE FIRST AUTO

Movie made in the USA in 1927 • Lobby card: USA • Size: 10x8in (25x20cm) • Rarity rating: 5
Motor: Oldsmobile? • Players: Russell Simpson, Barney Oldfield

Racer Barney Oldfield appeared in this movie, although that's Russell Simpson in – or on – what may well be an Oldsmobile

"THE FIRST AUTO" with BARNEY OLDFIELD — A Warner Bros. Production

SMASHING THROUGH

Movie made in the UK in 1928 • Poster: UK • Size: 18x12in (46x30cm) • Rarity rating: 4
• Motor: Artist's impression • Players: John Stuart, Alf Goddard, Eve Gray, Julie Suedo

Billed as "Britain's first great motor-racing picture" by Gaumont, which placed this trade advert in the August 30, 1928 issue of *Kinematograph Weekly*

NERVE

Movie made in Germany in 1929 • Poster: UK • Size: 18x12in (46x30cm)
Rarity rating: 4 • Motorcycle: Artist's impression • Players: Harry Peel, Vera Schmiterlow

Harry Peel was actually the multi-talented German, Harry Piel. As far as I can tell, this movie was originally titled *His Best Friend* for the German market. The poster is actually a trade advert from *Kinematograph Weekly* in which the studios informed distributors and in the cinemas of forthcoming attractions

AVENTURES À LISBONNE

Movie made in Germany
in 1930
Poster: Belgium
Size: 15x24in (38x61cm)
Rarity rating: 5
Motor: Mercedes-Benz
Players: Harry Piel

Harry Piel survived both world
wars as, variously, movie actor,
director, writer and producer

KÄRLEK OCH BENSIN

Movie made in Germany
in 1930
Poster: Sweden
Size: 28x39in (71x99cm)
Rarity rating: 5
Motor: Roadster
Players: Willy Fritsch, Lilian Harvey

Beautiful Art Deco Swedish poster, the title of which translates as Love and Petrol, taken from a German musical entitled *Drei Von Der Tankstelle*. The petrol pump emblem is genuine, the company is now run by Q8, previously Gulf

Le Bidon d'Or

Movie made in France in 1932 • Poster: France • Size: 94x63in (239x160cm) • Rarity rating: 5
Artist: Roger Cartier • Motor: Artist's impression • Players: Alex Nalpas, Raymond Cordy, Pierre Dac, Simone Bourday, Nicole Martel

Intriguingly, the title can mean 'gold cup', or 'piss pot': you choose ...

THE RACING STRAIN

Movie made in the USA in 1932
Poster: Belgium
Size: 24x34in (61x86cm)
Rarity rating: 5
Motor: Early racing chaos
Players: Wally Reid Jr, Mae Busch, Phyllis Barrington, Dickie Moore

A slight adaptation of the original American artwork to take in both French and Flemish titles

DIAVOLO L'INTRÉPIDE

Movie made in the USA in 1934 • Poster: France • Size: 60x96in (152x244cm) • Rarity rating: 5 • Motor: Ford • Players: Richard Talmadge

A magnificent piece for what was essentially a cinema serial

Pathé Consortium Cinéma *présente*

*du danger!
des luttes!
une course palpitante!*

PATHÉ-JOURNAL *Sonore et Parlant*

LE VIRAGE
DE LA MORT

FILM DIALOGUÉ *Français*
film ininflammable PATHÉ

avec FRANKIE DARRO
JACK MULHALL • LOLA LANE
JULIAN RIVERO • EDWIN MAXWELL
Réalisation
de Colbert CLARK et Armand SCHAEFER
Production MASCOT PICTURES

MARCEL

835.

AFFICHES GAILLARD - PARIS AMIENS - Procédé 35.

LE VIRAGE DE LA MORT

Movie made in the USA in 1934 • Poster: France • Size: 33x46in (84x117cm)
• Rarity rating: 5 • Artist: Marcel • Motor: Midget Racer

This was called *Burn 'em Up Barnes* in the USA, and starred Frankie Darro, Jack Mulhall
and Lola Lane

SABOTAGE

Movie made in the UK in 1936
Poster: India
Size: 27x40in (69x102cm)
Rarity rating: 2
Motor: Wolseley – artist's impression
Players: Alfred Hitchcock, Oscar Homolka, Sylvia Sidney, John Loder

A 1960s re-release poster of this Hitchcock thriller, showing the heart of London, a double-decker, and (probably) a Wolseley police car

SPEED REPORTER

Movie made in the USA in
1936
Poster: Italy
Size: 20x26in (51x66cm)
Rarity rating: 5
Artist: DeAngelus
Motor: Plymouth
Players: Richard Talmadge,
Luana Walters

Made in the USA as *Speed Reporter*. As with many of these posters, the car is frequently an 'artist's impression' of a vehicle, and therefore open to interpretation. Another way of saying I might be wrong ...

WILLIAM M. PIZOR
presents

Rich Relations

An IMPERIAL PRODUCTION

Printed in U. S. A.

RICH RELATIONS

Movie made in the USA in 1937 • Lobby card: USA • Size: 11x14in (28x36cm)
• Rarity rating: 5 • Motor: Packard • Players: Ralph Forbes, Frances Grant,
Barry Norton, Muriel Evans, Gertrude Astor

Hand-coloured lobby card, with what looks like a Packard cab, and a Harley-Davidson

WAR SAVINGS CAMPAIGN

TRAVELLING CINEMA VAN

UK Government campaign poster of 1939
Poster: UK
Size: 20x30in (51x76cm)
Rarity rating: 4
Motor: Thorneycroft

It sells entertainment; your money helps pay for the war. It's just the same today, but without the entertainment

OH JOHNNY, MON AMOUR

Movie made in the USA in 1940
Poster: Belgium
Size: 14x11in (36x28cm)
Rarity rating: 4
Motor: Artist's impression
Players: Tom Brown, Peggy Moran

A comedy musical with an elegant pink rag-top. The US title was *Johnny, How You Can Love*

21

COMÈTE BLONDE

Movie made in the USA in 1941
Poster: France
Size: 47x31in (119x79cm)
Rarity rating: 5
Artist: Albert Jorio
Motor: Dirt track racer
Players: Virginia Vale, Robert Kent, Barney Oldfield

"Blonde Comet" and a motor-racing heroine. Barney Oldfield did the serious stuff

IN FAST COMPANY

Movie made in the USA in 1946
Poster: Belgium
Size: 22x14in (56x36cm)
Rarity rating: 4
Motor: Artist's impression
Players: Leo Gorcey, Huntz Hall,
Bobby Jordan, Bowery Boys

Gorcey and Hall were famous
as "The Bowery Boys". Both the
French and Flemish titles feature
on the poster

MEMORIAS DE UN CHOFER DE TAXI

Movie made in Chile in 1946
Poster: Chile
Size: 30x43in (76x109cm)
Rarity rating: 5
Artist: Pepa
Motor: Taxi
Players: Lucho Cordoba

A strong resemblance here to the 'Johnnycab' driver in *Total Recall*, made over forty years later

THE BIG WHEEL

Movie made in the USA in 1949
Poster: Japan
Size: 20x29in (51x74cm)
Rarity rating: 4
Motor: Midget Racers
Players: Mickey Rooney

Mickey Rooney as ace racer

FANGIO

Movie made in Argentina in 1950
Poster: Argentina
Size: 27x42in (69x107cm)
Rarity rating: 5
Artist: RAF
Motor: Maserati
Players: Juan Manuel Fangio,
Armando Bo

Early bio-pic. Wonderful image of
Fangio in the Argentine-liveried
Maserati 4CLT, a car which still exists,
at the moment, in private hands. This
poster is thought to be one of just three
in the world; the location of each is
known

HI-JACKED

Movie made in the USA in 1950
Poster: USA
Size: 27x41in (69x104cm)
Rarity rating: 3
Motor: Fargo Truck (maybe)
Players: Jim Davis, Marsha Jones

I now expect hordes of letters from outraged Fargoistes, saying "nothing that ugly could be a Fargo"

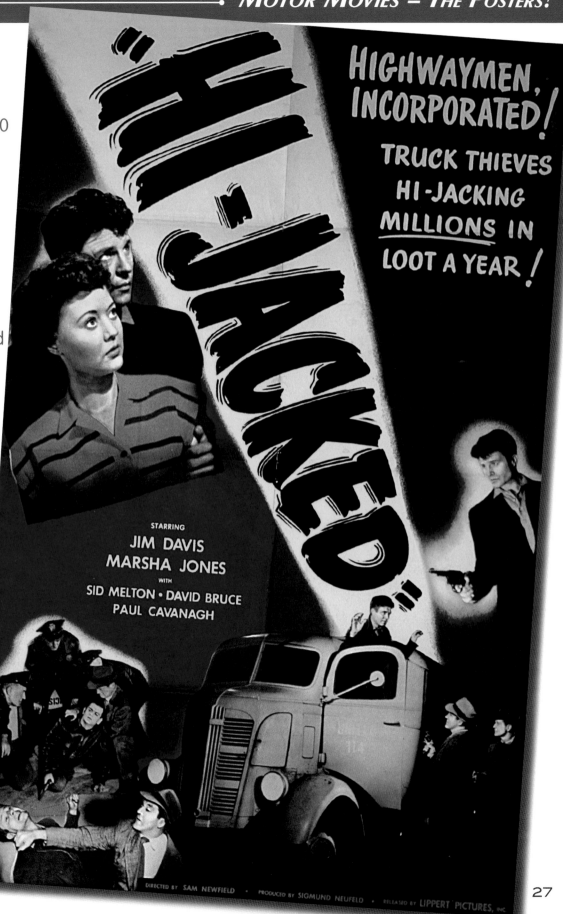

27

LE GANG DES TRACTIONS ARRIERE

Movie made in France in 1950
Poster: Belgium
Size: 22x14in (56x36cm)
Rarity rating: 3
Motor: Citroen – artist's impression
Players: Jean Paredes, Gustave Libeau, Raymond Cordy

Whatever the artist was on, it should be in the drinking water

MON AMI SAINFOIN

Movie made in France in 1950
Poster: France
Size: 47x63in (119x160cm)
Rarity rating: 4
Artist: Chavanne
Motor: Citroen 5CV
Players: Pierre Blanchar, Sophie Desmarets

A boldly colourful poster, but notice how the artist had lost interest by the time he reached the rear of the car

M·G·M's
Thrill-A-Minute
Romance!

CLARK GABLE ★ BARBARA STANWYCK

in TO PLEASE A LADY

ADOLPHE MENJOU
WILL GEER
Story and Screen Play by
BARRÉ LYNDON and MARGE DECKER
Produced and Directed by
CLARENCE BROWN
A METRO-GOLDWYN-MAYER PICTURE

50/579

TO PLEASE A LADY

Movie made in the USA in 1950 • Poster: USA • Size: 22x28in (56x71cm)
• Rarity rating: 4 • Motor: Midget Racers – artist's impression • Players: Clark
Gable, Barbara Stanwyck

Gable and Stanwyck are portrayed on this half-sheet. The movie was re-issued
in 1962 as *Red Hot Wheels*

WER FÜHR DEN GRAÜEN FORD?

Movie made in Germany in 1950
Poster: Germany
Size: 23x33in (58x84cm)
Rarity rating: 4
Motor: Ford
Players: Otto Wernicke, Ruth Hambrock, Erich Scholz, Ursula Herking

Little seen outside Germany, this translates as *Who's driving the grey Ford?*

31

PORTE D'ORIENT

Movie made in France in 1951
Poster: France
Size: 47x63in (119x160cm)
Rarity rating: 4
Artist: Yermel
Motor: Artist's impression
Players: Yves Vincent, Dalio, Nathalie Nattier, Tilda Thamar

Glorious poster: a little known film

LEA PADOVANI
PAOLA BARBARA
MARIA GRAZIA FRANCIA
JACQUES SERNAS
DARIO MICHAELIS
CHECCO DURANTE
BRUNA CORRÀ
DIANA LANTE
MARISA PALIANI
DINA SASSOLI
MARCELLO GIORDA
con la partecipazione di
ANTONELLA LUALDI
e del piccolo
AUGUSTO
★
Regìa:
MARIO BONNARD

I FIGLI NON SI VENDONO

Un film C.I. SCHERMI ASSOCIATI-ZEUS prodotto da ALBERTO MANCA

DISTRIBUZIONE

I FIGLI NON SI VENDONO

Movie made in Italy in 1952 • Poster: Italy • Size: 19x13in (48x33cm) • Rarity rating: 4 • Motor: Ferrari • Players: Antonella Lualdi, Lea Padovani, Paola Barbara

I'm not at all certain that this is actually a Ferrari, but it's a decent guess for this almost entirely unknown picture

THE PACE THAT THRILLS

Movie made in the USA in1952
Poster: USA
Size: 27x41in (69x104cm)
Rarity rating: 3
Motor: Race bikes
Players: Bill Williams, Carmen Balenda

TT and flat track racing effectively portrayed in this B-movie, with an all-action poster to match

TREFFPUNKT PARIS

Movie made in France in 1952
Poster: Germany
Size: 23x33in (58x84cm)
Rarity rating: 4
Motor: Artist's impression
Players: Marcel Andre,
Nicole Besnard,
Louis De Funes

AKA *Ils Etaient Cinq* (1952). Trying to decipher the artist's signature on this poster has exercised the great minds of the world. Well, mine, anyway

BACHELOR IN PARIS

Movie made in the UK in 1952
Poster: USA
Size: 27x41in (69x104cm)
Rarity rating: 3
Motor: Artist's impression of (probably) a Citroen Traction Cabrio
Players: Dennis Price, Hermione Baddeley, Anne Vernon, Mischa Auer

Known as *Song of Paris* when the movie was made in the UK in 1952; released in the USA as *Bachelor in Paris* in 1953. An excellent poster for Citroenistes and stocking fetishists alike

GENEVIEVE

Movie made in the UK in 1953 • Poster: UK
Size: 27x40in (69x102cm)
Rarity rating: 5 • Artist: Eric Pulford
Motor: Darracq • Players: John Gregson, Dinah Sheridan, Kaye Kendall, Kenneth More, William Rose, Henry Cornelius

The classic British tale of the Darracq and the Spyker on the Brighton Run resulted in this beautiful poster

GENEVIEVE

Movie made in the UK in 1953 • Poster: Spain
• Size: 4x6in (10x15cm) • Rarity rating: 4
• Motor: Darracq

This mini-poster, or flyer, packs a great deal into a very small space

JALOPY

Movie made in the USA in 1953
Poster: USA
Size: 27x41in (69x104cm)
Rarity rating: 4
Motor: Stock cars, or 'banger' racers
Players: Leo Gorcey, Huntz Hall, Bowery Boys

The handwriting on the bottom of this poster indicates it was used in Quebec

MUST I GET A DIVORCE?

Movie made in Germany in 1953
Poster: Germany
Size: 23x33in (58x84cm)
Rarity rating: 3
Artist: Gobel
Motor: Artist's impression
Players: Hardy Kruger,
Ruth Leuwerik

The racer has the look of Veritas or Mercedes, which was probably what Herr Gobel intended. Lovely portrait work of Hardy Kruger and Ruth Leuwerik

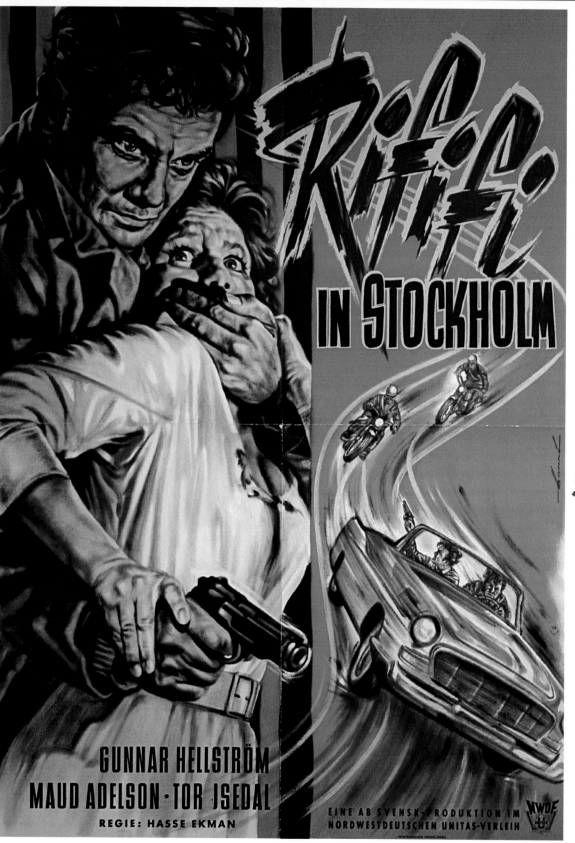

RIFIFI IN STOCKHOLM

Movie made in Sweden in 1953*
Poster: Germany
Size: 23x33in (58x84cm)
Rarity rating: 3
Artist: Heinz Bonne
Motor: Artist's impression
Players: Gunnar Hellstrom, Maud Adelson

The year of production is an educated guess for this virtually unknown movie. 'Rififi' translates from French as 'trouble'

*subsequently discovered to be 1961

40

TAXI

Movie made in the USA in 1953
Poster: USA
Size: 14x36in (36x91cm)
Rarity rating: 3
Motor: De Soto
Players: Dan Dailey, Constance Smith

The De Soto has been residing in the same Dutch museum as the Darracq and the Spyker from *Genevieve*

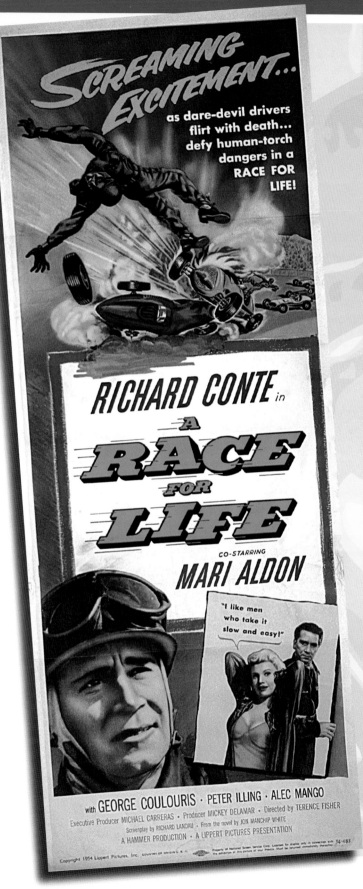

A RACE FOR LIFE

Movie made in the UK in 1954
Poster: USA
Size: 14x36in (36x91cm)
Rarity rating: 3
Motor: Talbot-Lago – artist's impression
Players: Richard Conte, Stirling Moss, Reg Parnell, John Cooper

Richard Conte starred in this English production, known in the UK as *Mask of Dust*. Stirling Moss, Reg Parnell, and John Cooper all had active roles

JOHNNY DARK

Movie made in the USA in 1954
Poster: USA
Size: 14x36in (36x91cm)
Rarity rating: 3
Motor: Allard – artist's impression
Players: Tony Curtis, Piper Laurie, Don Taylor

A radical race car, a daring dame, reckless rivals, and a miserable millionaire ... what more do you want?

JOHNNY DARK

Movie made in the USA in 1954 • Poster: France
Size: 47x63in (119x160cm) • Rarity rating: 4 • Artist: Noel
Motor: Perhaps Allard – artist's impression
Spectacular – if slightly odd – choice of colour scheme

THE FAST AND THE FURIOUS

Movie made in the USA in 1954 • Poster: UK • Size: • 30x40in (76x102cm) • Rarity rating: 4 • Motor: Jaguar
Players: Dorothy Malone, John Ireland

Proof that nothing is new, in a movie that had the look of an extended XK120 commercial

DU GRAIN POUR LES POULETS

Movie made in Spain in 1955
Poster: France
Size: 47x63in (119x160cm)
Rarity rating: 4
Artist: Belinsky
Motor: Citroen Traction
Players: Jacques Avellan, Louis Induni

No amount of research has revealed the exact year of production for this movie, but a reasonably informed guess would be mid-1950s

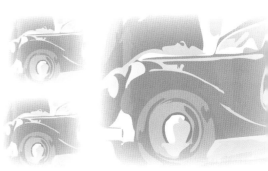

REBEL WITHOUT A CAUSE

Movie made in the USA in 1955
Poster: Sweden
Size: 28x12in (71x30cm)
Rarity rating: 4
Artist: Unknown
Motor: Ford Mercury
Players: James Dean

Great photo portrait of James Dean

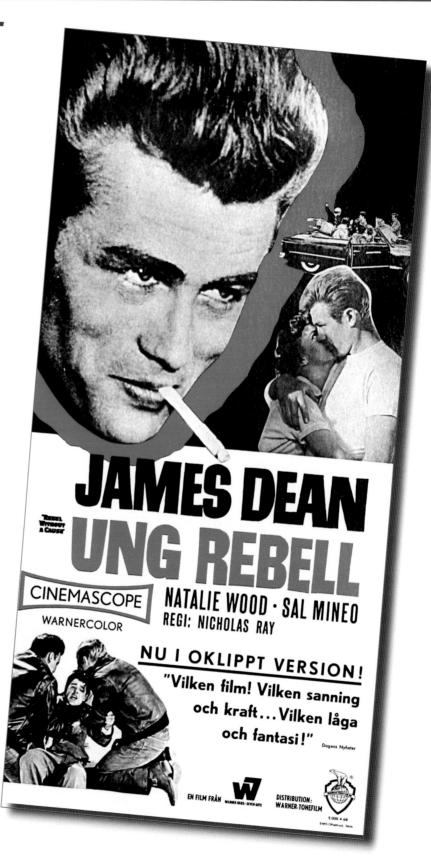

THE RACERS

Movie made in the USA in 1955
Poster: France
Size: 14x30in (36x76cm)
Rarity rating: 4
Motor: Artist's impression
Players: Kirk Douglas, Bella Darvi, Gilbert Roland

Unusual format, and great artwork

47

THE RACERS

Movie made in the USA
in 1955
Poster: Czechoslovakia
Size: 20x27in (51x69cm)
Rarity rating: 4
Artist: A L
Motor: Alfa Romeo – artist's
impression
Players: Simon Taylor, Kirk Douglas,
Bella Darvi, Gilbert Roland

The mysterious A L gives a completely
different take on this Czech poster
for *The Racers*, a movie – as you can
see – of many different names. The
British release was titled *Such Men
are Dangerous*

THE RACERS

Movie made in the USA in 1955
Poster: Belgium
Size: 22x14in (56x36cm)
Rarity rating: 3
Motor: HWM, Stovebolt Special, Talbot-Lago – artist's impression
Players: Kirk Douglas, Bella Darvi, Gilbert Roland, Simon Taylor

Wonderful artwork, as on many Belgian posters from this period. The HWM on the
left is still being campaigned in Europe as the fearsome 'Stovebolt Special',
by motoring scribe, Simon Taylor

CASH ON DELIVERY

Movie made in the UK in 1956 • Lobby card: USA • Size: 10x8in (25x20cm) Rarity rating: 3 • Motor: Austin-Healey • Players: John Gregson, Shelley Winters

Originally titled *To Dorothy A Son*, this version starred John Gregson and Shelley Winters

CHECKPOINT

Movie made in the UK in 1956
Poster: UK
Size: 30x40in (76x102cm)
Rarity rating: 4
Motor: Aston Martin DB3S
Players: Stanley Baker, Anthony Steel,
Odile Versois, James Robertson-Justice

Actually, an artist's impression of a bodged body of a DB3S, so you could be forgiven for not recognising it. This was the poster that changed my life, mostly by making me very much poorer ...

CHECKPOINT

Movie made in the UK in 1957
Poster: Japan
Size: 20x29in (51x74cm)
Rarity rating: 3
Motor: Alfa Romeo, Ferrari, Porsche

Criminal enterprise set against the Mille Miglia. A slightly later release in Japan than in the UK

CHECKPOINT

Movie made in the UK in 1956 • Lobby card: UK
Size: 11x14in (28x36cm) • Rarity rating: 3
Motor: Aston Martin

Purporting to be the famous DB3S, but with a most unhappy nose job

COME NEXT SPRING

Movie made in the USA in 1956
Poster: Italy
Size: 26x18in (66x46cm)
Rarity rating: 4
Motor: Ford
Players: Steve Cochran, Ann Sheridan

The Italian title translates as "The Greatest Love in the World". Steve Cochran falls for a Model T – and Ann Sheridan

HOT CARS

Movie made in the USA in 1956
Poster: USA
Size: 27x41in (69x104cm)
Rarity rating: 2
Motor: Artist's impression
Players: John Bromfield, Carol Shannon, Joi Lansing

'A stop-at-nothing blonde; a buck-hungry guy …'. Not just art; but literature, too

53

LE CIRCUIT DE MINUIT

Movie made in Belgium in 1956
Poster: France
Size: 47x63in (119x160cm)
Rarity rating: 3
Artist: Brenot
Lancia Ferrari – artist's impression
Players: Blanchette Brunoy, Yves Vincent, Albert Prejean, Luc Varenne

Very rare to see this Grand Prix car in any movie-related publicity

NOT SO DUSTY

Movie made in the UK in 1956 • Poster: UK • Size: 30x40in (76x102cm) • Rarity rating: 4
• Motor: Dust cart, garbage truck • Players: Joy Nichols, Bill Owen, Leslie Dwyer

This makes up for in jolliness what it lacks in the exotic

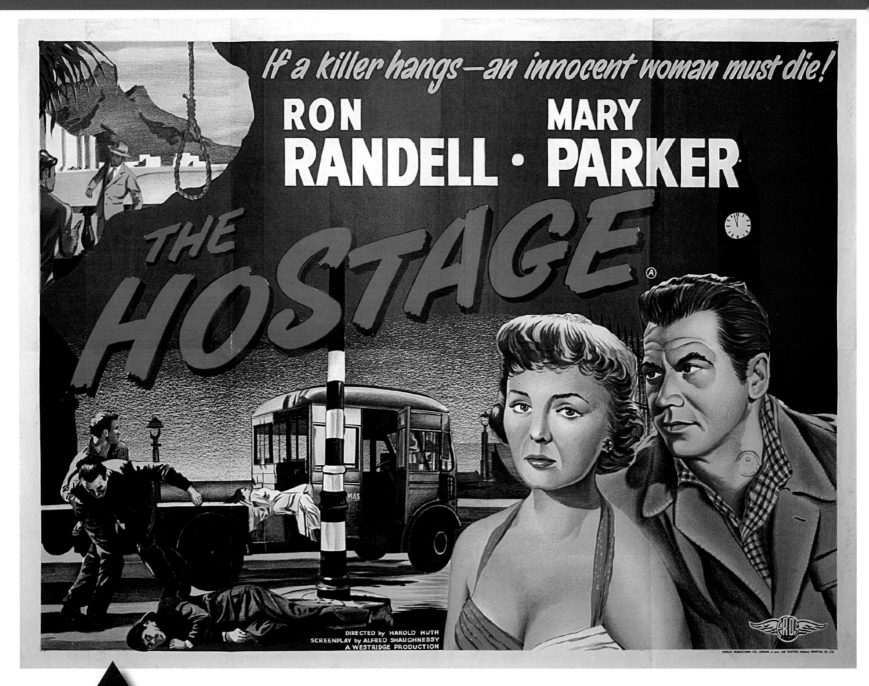

THE HOSTAGE

Movie made in the UK in 1956 • Poster: UK • Size: 30x40in (76x102cm) • Rarity rating: 4
Motor: Unusual crew cab truck • Players: Ron Randell, Mary Parker

Lovely artwork for a largely unloved movie

THE SOLID GOLD CADILLAC

Movie made in the USA in 1956
Poster: USA
Size: 27x41in (69x104cm)
Rarity rating: 3
Motor: Cadillac
Players: Judy Holliday, Paul Douglas

Judy Holliday was perfect for the ditzy blonde on the Eldorado

57

WARNER BROS. PICTURES, INC. *Presents* A DOUGLAS FAIRBANKS, JR. PRODUCTION "CHASE A CROOKED SHADOW" STARRING RICHARD TODD · ANNE BAXTER · HERBERT LOM

Screenplay by DAVID OSBORN and CHARLES SINCLAIR
Directed by MICHAEL ANDERSON

PROPERTY OF NATIONAL SCREEN SERVICE CORP. LICENSED FOR DISPLAY ONLY IN CONNECTION WITH THE EXHIBITION OF THIS PICTURE AT YOUR THEATRE. MUST BE RETURNED IMMEDIATELY THEREAFTER.

COPYRIGHT 1958 WARNER BROS. PICTURES DISTRIBUTING CORPORATION. PERMISSION GRANTED FOR NEWSPAPERS AND MAGAZINE REPRODUCTION. MADE IN U.S.A.

58/105

CHASE A CROOKED SHADOW

Movie made in the UK in 1957 • Lobby card: USA • Size: 10x8in (25x20cm) • Rarity rating: 3
Motor: Lagonda • Players: Richard Todd, Anne Baxter, Herbert Lom

A fine thriller, but the show was stolen by the Lagonda

Hollywood's Newest
TEENAGE STARS:

FAY SPAIN

STEVE TERRELL

JOHN ASHLEY

FRANK GORSHIN

DRAGSTRIP GIRL

An AMERICAN-INTERNATIONAL Picture

A GOLDEN STATE PRODUCTION • Produced by ALEX GORDON • Executive Producer: SAMUEL Z. ARKOFF • Screenplay by LOU RUSOFF • Directed by EDWARD L. CAHN

COPYRIGHT 1957 AMERICAN INTERNATIONAL PICTURES   COUNTRY OF ORIGIN U.S.A.

Property of National Screen Service Corp. Licensed for display only in connection with the exhibition of this picture at your theatre. Must be returned immediately thereafter.

57 127

DRAGSTRIP GIRL

Movie made in the USA in 1957 • Lobby card: USA • Size: 11x14in (28x36cm)
Rarity rating: 3 • Motor: Ford Hot Rods • Players: Frank Gorshin, John Ashley, Steve Terrell, Fay Spain, Samuel Z Arkoff

This lobby card is one of a set of eight

Parents
may
be
shocked
but...
YOUTH
WILL
UNDERSTAND!

AB-PT PICTURES CORPORATION presents

Eighteen and Anxious

starring

WILLIAM CAMPBELL · MARTHA SCOTT · JACKIE LOUGHERY · JIM BACKUS · RON HAGERTHY · JACKIE COOGAN and MARY WEBSTER as the girl who is Eighteen and Anxious

Executive Producer IRVING H. LEVIN · Produced by EDMOND CHEVIE · Directed by JOE PARKER
Screenplay by DALE and KATHERINE EUNSON
Distributed by REPUBLIC PICTURES CORPORATION

Property of National Screen Service Corp. Licensed for display only in connection with the exhibition of this picture at your theatre. Must be returned immediately thereafter.

4

57/586

COUNTRY OF ORIGIN U.S.A.

EIGHTEEN AND ANXIOUS

Movie made in the USA in 1957 • Lobby card: USA • Size: 14x11in (36x28cm)
Rarity rating: 2 • Motor: Triumph, Jaguar, MG, Austin-Healey • Players: William
Campbell, Martha Scott, Jackie Coogan

Angst-ridden American youth in classic British sports cars. No wonder they were
anxious ...

HELL DRIVERS

Movie made in the UK in 1957
Poster: UK
Size: 40x27in (102x69cm)
Rarity rating: 5
Artist: Angelo Cesselon
Motor: Trucks, actually
Players: Stanley Baker, Herbert Lom, Patrick McGoohan, Peggy Cummins, William Hartnell, Sid James, Sean Connery, Jill Ireland, Alfie Bass, Gordon Kackson, Wilfred Lawson

Hell Drivers has acquired a cult following in the past few years, as much for its crazed, undercranked trucking action as its heavyweight cast

61

LA COLUMBIA PICTURES *presenta*

HOMICIDAL

GLENN CORBETT
PATRICIA BRESLIN
EUGENIE LEONTOVICH • ALAN BUNCE
JAMES WESTERFIELD
e JEAN ARLESS

AVVERTENZA *Il diritto di utilizzare la presente fotobusta è riservato esclusivamente al Cliente che ne ha fatto diretto acquisto dalla S.A.C. - S.p.A. - Le infrazioni saranno perseguite a norma di legge*

Soggetto di ROBB WHITE • *Prodotto e diretto da* WILLIAM CASTLE • *Una produzione* WILLIAM CASTLE

HOMICIDAL

Movie made in the USA in 1957 • Poster: Italy • Size: 26x18in (66x46cm) • Rarity rating: 3
Motor: Ford Fairlane • Players: Glen Corbett, Jean Arless, Patricia Breslin

These Italian photobustas are the equivalent of the lobby card, available in sets of six or more

PROGRES FILMS

UN FILM DE
EEN FILM VAN A. RADOK

avec 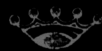 met

RAYMOND BUSSIERES

ANNETTE POIVRE

GINETTE PIGEON

texte de / dit par
tekst van / gesproken door

Camille FICHEFET | Luc VARENNE

LES ROIS DE
LA VITESSE

DE KONINGEN DER SNELHEID

LES ROIS DE LA VITESSE

Movie made in Czechoslovakia in 1957
Poster: Belgium
Size: 14x21in (36x53cm)
Rarity rating: 3
Motor: Early racers
Players: Raymond Bussieres, Luc Varenne, Annette Poivre

Translating as *The Kings of Speed*, this comedy was based on the early days of motor racing

TEEN AGE THUNDER

Movie made in the USA in 1957 • Poster: USA • Size: 27x41in (69x104cm) • Rarity rating: 3 • Motor: Ford Hot Rod
Players: Charles Courtney, Melinda Byron, Robert Fuller

Very desirable poster for what is now a cult movie

TEEN AGE THUNDER

Movie made in the USA in 1957
Poster: USA
Size: 22x28in (56x71cm)
Rarity rating: 3
Motor: Ford Hot Rod

This half-sheet is an even better bet than the larger one sheet

THE DEVIL'S HAIRPIN

Movie made in the USA in 1957
Poster: Argentina
Size: 27x42in (69x107cm)
Rarity rating: 4
Motor: Jaguar D-Type, Aston Martin DB3S, Arnolt-Bristol, and Chuck Porter's Mercedes-Benz 300SLS
Players: Cornel Wilde, Jean Wallace

Cornel Wilde did pretty much everything in this movie, including turning Chuck Porter's very pretty Mercedes into the yellow beast pictured here

65

THE MAN IN THE ROAD

Movie made in the UK in 1957 • Poster: USA • Size: 22x28in (56x71cm) • Rarity rating: 3
Motor: Humber Hawk • Players: Derek Farr, Ella Raines, Donald Wolfit, Cyril Cusack

Commie agents foiled by the good old British bobby in his trusty Humber

INCOGNITO

Movie made in France in 1958
Poster: France
Size: 47x63in (119x160cm)
Rarity rating: 4
Artist: Basarte
Motor: Chevrolet Corvette
Players: Eddie Constantine, Tilda
Thamar

The famous detective upstaged by
the early Corvette

MADAME ET SON AUTO

Movie made in France in 1958
Poster: Belgium
Size: 14x21in (36x53cm)
Rarity rating: 2
Motor: Citroen
Players: Sophie Desmarets

A ripple bonnet 2CV starred with Sophie Desmarets

CARRERA MORTAL

Movie made in the USA in
1959
Poster: Argentina
Size: 27x42in (69x107cm)
Rarity rating: 4
Motor: Austin-Healey Special,
MGTF, Ferrari
Players: Yvonne Lime, Slick
Slavin, Brett Halsey, Charles Willcox

Cult US movie called *Speed Crazy*. An early poster example of the now cliched 'car-between-the-legs' routine

IN DIE FALLE GELOCK

Movie made in France in 1959
Poster: Germany
Size: 23x33in (58x84cm)
Rarity rating: 4
Motor: Ferrari 250
Players: Bernard Borderie,
Antonella Lualdi, Felix Marten,
Falco Lulli

A French take on an Italian
car-driving British detective for
the German market

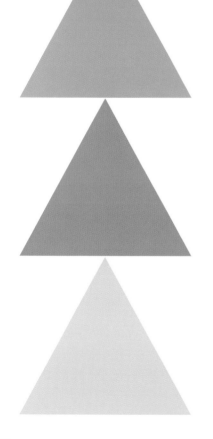

MADEMOISELLE ANGE

Movie made in France in 1959
Poster: France
Size: 47x63in (119x160cm)
Rarity rating: 4
Artist: Hurel
Motor: Race car caricature
Players: Romy Schneider, Jean-Paul Belmondo, Henri Vidal

The pronounced fold lines are a result of machine folding prior to distribution, then 45 years of folded storage

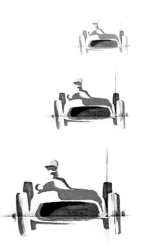

MATCH CONTRE LA MORT

Movie made in France in 1959
Poster: France
Size: 16x23in (41x58cm)
Rarity rating: 4
Artist: Yves Thos
Motor: Panhard
Players: Antonella Lualdi, Gerard Blain

Motoring scribe, Ed McDonough, tells me it's a Panhard; I'm still leaning towards Bonnet. Yves Thos is an acclaimed French artist, responsible for some superb cinema artwork

MON POTE LE GITAN

Movie made in France in 1959
Poster: France
Size: 23x30in (58x76cm)
Rarity rating: 3
Artist: David
Motor: Caricature
Players: Louis De Funes, Jean Richard

I was glad there was a car of sorts in this, but David's Vargas-like lady was the real appeal

T-BIRD GANG

Movie made in the USA in 1959
Poster: USA
Size: 27x41in (69x104cm)
Rarity rating: 2
Artist: R Besser
Motor: Ford Thunderbird
Players: John Brinkley, Pat George, Ed Nelson

Deliberately cheap-looking, but highly effective poster

GHOST OF DRAGSTRIP HOLLOW

Movie made in the USA in 1959
Poster: USA
Size: 27x41in (69x104cm)
Rarity rating: 4
Motor: Ford
Players: Jody Fair, Martin Braddock, Russ Bender

A cult hot-rodding movie, and a rapidly appreciating poster

TOO MANY CROOKS

Movie made in UK in 1959
Poster: Italy
Size: 13x27in (33x69cm)
Rarity rating: 4
Motor: Toon
Players: Sid James, Terry-Thomas, George Cole, Bernard Bresslaw, Brenda De-Banzi, Mario Zampi

Classic British comedy, and delightful Italian caricature poster

LES FIANCÉS DE LA MORT

Movie made in Italy • Poster: France • Size: 47x63in (119x160cm) • Rarity rating: 3 • Artist: DeAmicis Motor: Racing bikes

Big name racers and the beautiful Sylva Koscina

LES FIANCÉS DE LA MORT

Movie made in Italy in 1960 • Poster: France • Size: 23x30in (58x76cm) • Rarity rating: 3 • Artist: DeAmicis • Motor: Racing motorcycles • Players: Sylva Koscina, Geoff Duke, Pierre Monneret, Bill Lomas, Enrico Lorenzetti, Libero Liberati

Fidanzati Della Morte originally, this had a host of top name bikers such as Geoff Duke, Pierre Monneret, Libero Liberati, Bill Lomas, Enrico Lorenzetti, and others, to offset the beautiful Sylva Koscina

THE LEAGUE OF GENTLEMEN

Movie made in the UK in 1960 • Poster: UK • Size: 20x30in (51x76cm) • Rarity rating: 4
Motor: Standard Vanguard • Players: Jack Hawkins, Nigel Patrick, Richard Attenborough, Robert Coote, Roger Livesey

Technically, not a movie poster at all, but a tie-in between Allied Film Makers and Standard: "the car all Gentlemen prefer"

From roaring hot rods...
to the
racing
big time

THE WILD RIDE

starring
JACK NICHOLSON
GEORGIANNA CARTER

Produced and Directed by HARVEY BERMAN
Executive Producer KINTA ZERTUCHE
Screenplay by ANN PORTER and MARION ROTHMAN
A FILMGROUP PRESENTATION

THE WILD RIDE

Movie made in the USA in 1960
Poster: USA
Size: 27x41in (69x104cm)
Rarity rating: 3
Motor: Hot Rod and Indy racer
– artist's impression
Players: Jack Nicholson

Early Jack Nicholson role. To the left of the racer is the Quebec censor's stamp

A MATTER OF WHO

Movie made in UK in 1961 • Lobby card: USA • Size: 11x14in (28x36cm) • Rarity rating: 3 • Motor: Austin Seven
Players: Terry-Thomas

Terry-Thomas emerges from under a Mann truck

L'Urlo Dei Bolidi

Movie made in Italy in 1961 • Poster: Italy • Size: 27x18in (69x46cm) • Rarity rating: 4 • Motor: De Sanctus, and perhaps a Lister? • Players: Bella Darvi, Perez Prado, Walter Santesso, Rossana Rossanigo

A rough translation is *The Roar of the Racers*. It had a small release in UK where it was known as *The Roar of The Bolidi*

THE BIG GAMBLE

Movie made in the USA in 1961 • Poster: UK • Size: 30x40in (76x102cm) • Rarity rating: 4 • Artist: Tom Chantrell
Motor: Anonymous truck • Players: Darryl F Zanuck, Stephen Boyd, Juliette Greco, David Wayne

Beautiful Chantrell artwork for a seldom-seen movie

THE GREEN HELMET

Movie made in the UK in 1961 • Poster: USA • Size: 22x28in (56x71cm) • Rarity rating: 3 • Motor: Maserati, Ferrari
Players: Bill Travers, Jack Brabham, Sidney James, Ed Begley

The Birdcage, in various colours, took the lead in most publicity for this movie

THE GREEN HELMET

Movie made in the UK in 1961 • Poster: Italy • Size: 55x39in (140x99cm) • Rarity rating: 3 • Artist: Nano • Motor: Maserati, Ferrari

The Birdcage gets all the kudos, but the hero mostly drove a Lister-Jaguar

THE GREEN HELMET

Movie made in the UK in 1961 • Poster: Belgium • Size: 23x16in (58x41cm)
Rarity rating: 3 • Motor: Maserati, Ferrari

The Maserati Birdcage artwork was pretty much standard worldwide, with just colour and peripherals differing, country to country

BON VOYAGE

Movie made in the USA in 1962
Poster: USA
Size: 27x41in (69x104cm)
Rarity rating: 2
Motor: Citroen Traction
Players: Fred MacMurray, Jane Wyman, Jessie Royce Landis

You don't have to be fond of this movie to enjoy the sights of Paris in the early 1960s

THE FAST LADY

Movie made in the UK in 1962 • Poster: UK • Size: 30x40in (76x102cm) • Rarity rating: 3
Motor: Bentley • Players: Leslie Phillips, Stanley Baxter, James Robertson-Justice, Julie Christie

THE FAST LADY

Movie made in the UK in 1962 • Poster: Sweden
Size: 27x39in (69x99cm) • Rarity rating: 3
Artist: Bjorne • Motor: Bentley

The Leslie Phillips caricature is from the British artwork, but the Bentley 3-litre and the scantily clad ladies are the work of the Swedish artist; bless him

THE FAST LADY

Movie made in the UK in 1962 • Poster: France • Size: 10x8in (25x20cm) • Rarity rating: 3 • Motor: Morris Mini-Cooper

Julie Christie adorns the Mini's nose, in her first 'gai' role; in this instance, 'gai' translates as 'comedy'

I DIAVOLO DEL GRAND PRIX

Movie made in the USA in 1963
Poster: Italy
Size: 55x39in (140x99cm)
Rarity rating: 3
Motor: Ferrari – artist's impression
Players: Roger Corman, Mark Damon, William Campbell

This is *The Young Racers* in its 1970 Italian release

L'IRRÉSISTIBLE CÉLIBATAIRE

Movie made in Germany in 1963
Poster: France
Size: 47x63in (119x160cm)
Rarity rating: 3
Artist: Tealdi
Motor: Citroen 2CV
Players: Francois Prevost, Alexandra Stewart

AKA *A Man at His Best Age*

PARANOIAC

Movie made in the UK in 1963
Poster: France
Size: 47x63in (119x160cm)
Rarity rating: 3
Artist: Belinsky
Motor: MG
Players: Oliver Reed, Janette Scott, Sheila Burrell

The Evil-Eye Fleagle look from Olly Read, beautifully captured by one of France's top poster artists

THE CHECKERED FLAG

Movie made in the USA in 1963
Poster: USA
Size: 27x41in (69x104cm)
Rarity rating: 3
Motor: Artist's impression
Players: Joe Morrison, Evelyn King

Very basic poster which has grown in desirability over the past few years

THE YOUNG RACERS

Movie made in the USA in 1963
Poster: USA
Size: 27x41in (69x104cm)
Rarity rating: 3
Motor: Race cars – artist's impression
Players: Bruce McLaren, Jim Clark, Roger Corman, Mark Damon

The wonderful Roger Corman with "A little death each day, a lot of love every night." However, the cars were real (mostly), and Bruce McLaren and Jim Clark made appearances

ÉCHAPPEMENT LIBRE

Movie made in France in 1964
Poster: Italy
Size: 75x54in (191x137cm)
Rarity rating: 4
Artist: Brini
Motor: Triumph TR4
Players: Jean-Paul Belmondo, Jean Seberg, Fernando Rey, Gert Frobe

Smuggling? Well of course you'd use a solid gold TR4. AKA *Backfire*

RACING FEVER

Movie made in the USA in 1964
Poster: USA
Size: 27x41in (69x104cm)
Rarity rating: 2
Motor: De Floto?
Players: Joe Morrison, Gerry Granahan, Barbara Biggart

Motors don't need wheels, as this outstanding poster featuring power boat racing demonstrates

VERFÜHRUNG AM STRAND

Movie made in Argentina in 1964 • Poster: Germany • Size: 46x32in (117x81cm) • Rarity rating: 4
Artist: Rehak • Motor: Artist's impression • Players: Alberto De Mendoza, Susana Freyre

The car looks like a cross between a C-Type Jaguar, and a Mercedes-Benz. In Argentina the film was called *Primero Yo*, and in the UK *Me First*

VIVA LAS VEGAS

Movie made in the USA in 1964
Poster: France
Size: 47x63in (119x160cm)
Rarity rating: 3
Artist: Soubie
Motor: Race cars
– artist's impression
Players: Elvis Presley, Ann-Margret

Elvis, Ann-Margret, and fast cars. Perfection

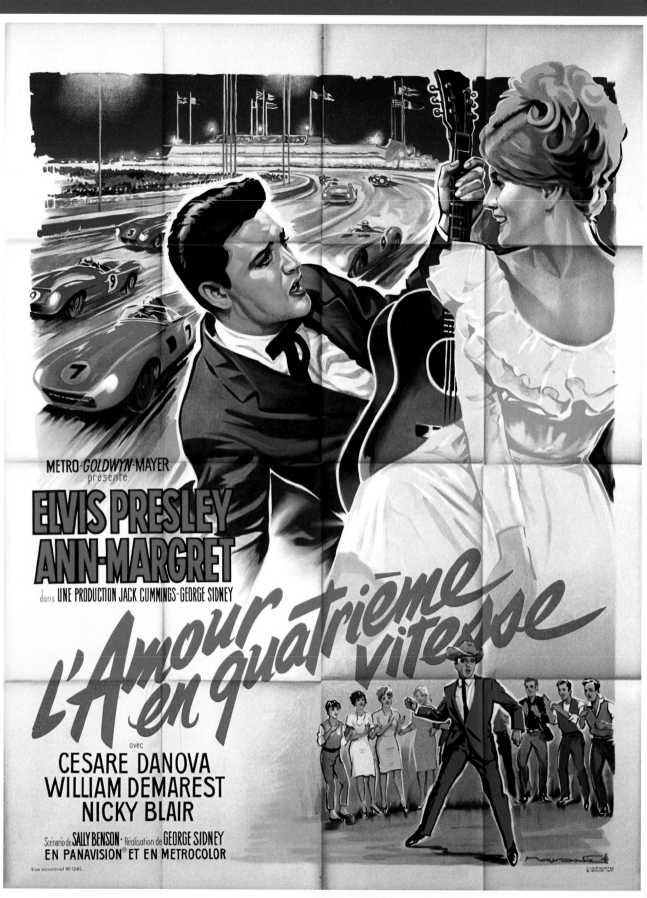

FASTER PUSSYCAT! KILL! KILL!

Movie made in the USA in 1965 • Lobby card: France
Size: 12x10in (30x25cm) • Rarity rating: 4
Motor: Porsche

Russ Meyer's ode to feminism, or a cult offering of female violence and sports cars, depending on your point of view. Haji, Tura Satana, and Lori Williams featured prominently

FASTER PUSSYCAT! KILL! KILL!

Movie made in the USA in 1965 • Poster: Germany
Size: 23x33in (58x84cm) • Rarity rating: 3
Motor: MGB • Players: Russ Meyer, Haji, Tura Satana, Lori Williams

The outrageous Russ Meyer, tipped over the edge in German translation

LA COMMUNALE

Movie made in France in 1965
Poster: France
Size: 23x30 in (58x76cm)
Rarity rating: 3
Artist: Bourduge
Motor: Peugeot 301
Players: Robert Dhery, Colette Brosset, Didier Haudepin, Yves Robert

AKA *Public School*

RED LINE 7000

Movie made in the USA in 1965 • Lobby card: USA • Size: 10x8in (25x20cm) • Rarity rating: 3 • Motor: AC Cobra Daytona Players: Howard Hawks, James Caan

RED LINE 7000

Movie made in the USA in 1965 • Poster: France Size: 47x63in (119x160cm) • Rarity rating: 3 Artist: Soubie • Motor: Stock car – artist's impression

Howard Hawks' take on motor racing, which introduced James Caan to a wider world

THE SUCKER

Movie made in France in 1965
Poster: Sweden
Size: 39x27in (99x69cm)
Rarity rating: 2
Motor: Cadillac, Jaguar, Rolls-Royce
Players: Louis De Funes, Bourvil

Initially known as *Le Corniaud* in France

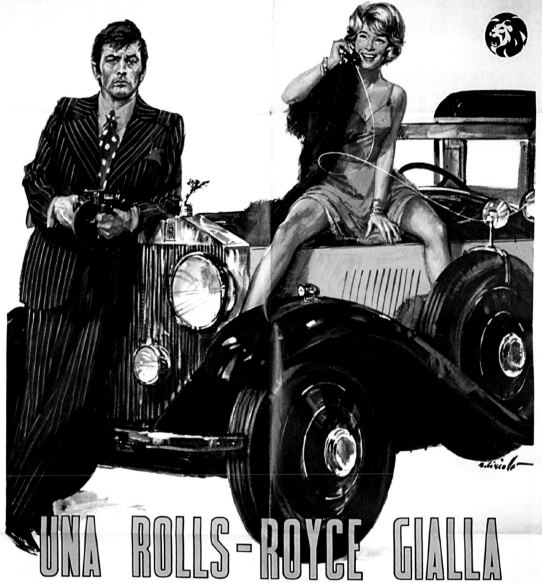

THE YELLOW ROLLS-ROYCE

Movie made in the UK in 1965
Poster: Italy
Size: 55x39in (140x99cm)
Rarity rating: 3
Artist: Ciriello
Motor: Rolls-Royce
Players: Alain Delon, Rex Harrison, Ingrid Bergman, George C Scott, Jeanne Moreau, Shirley MacLaine

A wonderful cast translates Terence Rattigan's story

TRAIN D'ENFER

Movie made in France in 1965
Poster: France
Size: 47x63in (119x160cm)
Rarity rating: 3
Artist: Allard
Motor: Alfa Romeo
Players: Jean Marais, Melissa Mell

Allard must have been an Alfa enthusiast to pay so much attention to the grille badge

WHITE LIGHTNIN' ROAD

Movie made in the USA in 1965
Poster: USA
Size: 27x41in (69x104cm)
Rarity rating: 3
Motor: Stock cars – artist's impression
Players: Arlene Hunter, Earl 'Snake' Richards

Fabulously trashy poster with crude stock cars and moonshiners, but the copywriter had a ball: "Souped Up Cars and Barnyard Babes"; "Ruby Wanted a Bang-Up Wedding, so her Pappa used his Shotgun!". And the movie itself? Anything this over-the-top has to be worth hunting down

CALIFORNIA HOLIDAY

Movie made in the USA in 1966
Poster: Italy
Size: 55x39in (140x99cm)
Rarity rating: 4
Artist: di Stefano
Motor: Race car – artist's impression
Players: Elvis Presley, Shelley Fabares, Deborah Walley, Diane McBain, Norman Taurog

Also known as *Spinout*

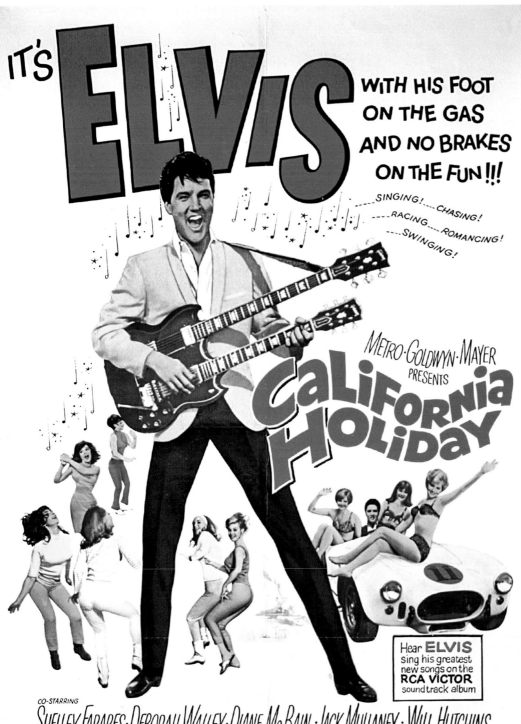

CALIFORNIA HOLIDAY

Movie made in the USA in 1966
Poster: USA
Size: 27x41in (69x104cm)
Rarity rating: 3
Motor: AC Cobra
Players: Elvis Presley, Diane McBain,
Norman Taurog, Shelley Fabares,
Deborah Walley

Also released as *Spinout*

FIREBALL 500

Movie made in the USA in 1966
Poster: USA
Size: 27x41in (69x104cm)
Rarity rating: 3
Motor: US Stock Car Racers
Players: Samuel Z Arkoff, Frankie
Avalon, Annette Funicello, Fabian,
Chill Wills

A cast designed to appeal to those
crazy rock & roll kids

GRAND PRIX

Movie made in the USA in 1966
Poster: UK • Size: 30x40in
(76x102cm) • Rarity rating: 5
Motor: Artist's impression
Players: James Garner, John
Frankenheimer, Brian Bedford,
Jessica Walter, Yves Montand,
Francoise Hardy, Eva-Marie Sainte,
Toshiro Mifune, Adolfo Celi

Image was unique to the UK poster

GRAND PRIX

Movie made in the USA in 1966 • Poster: France
Size: 47x63in (119x160cm) • Rarity rating: 4 •
Artist: Landi • Motor: Racing – artist's impression

Exceptional artwork from one of the world's top
poster artists

GRAND PRIX

Movie made in the USA in 1966
Poster: Japan
Size: 20x29in (51x74cm) Rarity
rating: 3
Motor: F1 Honda mock-up

One of several posters made
for this movie by the Japanese,
understandably, given the
Honda connection. Note
the interesting treatment of
Garner-san's portrait ...

HOW TO STEAL A MILLION

Movie made in the USA in 1966
Poster: USA
Size: 27x41in (69x104cm)
Rarity rating: 3
Motor: Jaguar E-Type
Players: Peter O'Toole, Audrey Hepburn, Eli Wallach, William Wyler, Charles Boyer, Hugh Griffith

A pity that this should be unsigned by the artist as these are wonderful portraits of Audrey Hepburn and Peter O'Toole

LE CHIEN FOU

Movie made in France in 1966
Poster: France
Size: 47x63in (119x160cm)
Rarity rating: 3
Artist: Jouineau-Bourduge
Motor: Ford Mustang
Players: Claude Brasseur, Dany Carrel

AKA *The Mad Dog* (UK/USA)

L'HOMME À LA FERRARI

Movie made in Italy in 1966
Poster: France
Size: 47x63in (119x160cm)
Rarity rating: 3
Artist: Oussenko
Motor: Ferrari
Players: Ann-Margret, Vittorio Gassman, Eleanor Parker

Ann Margret AND a Ferrari. Heaven. AKA *Il Tigre*

THE GLASS BOTTOMED BOAT

Movie made in the USA in 1966
Poster: Japan
Size: 20x29in (51x74cm)
Rarity rating: 4
Motor: Jaguar
Players: Doris Day, Rod Taylor

Also known as *The Spy in Lace Panties*. Double-O-Doris just doesn't have the same ring, somehow

UN HOMME ET UNE FEMME

Movie made in France in 1966
Poster: Japan
Size: 20x29in (51x74cm)
Rarity rating: 4
Motor: Ford GT40
Players: Claude Lelouch, Anouk Aimee, Jean-Louis Trintignant

Claude Lelouch directed Anouk Aimee and Jean-Louis Trintignant in this, one of the great romantic movies. Jean-Louis was nephew to successful race drivers Louis and Maurice Trintignant

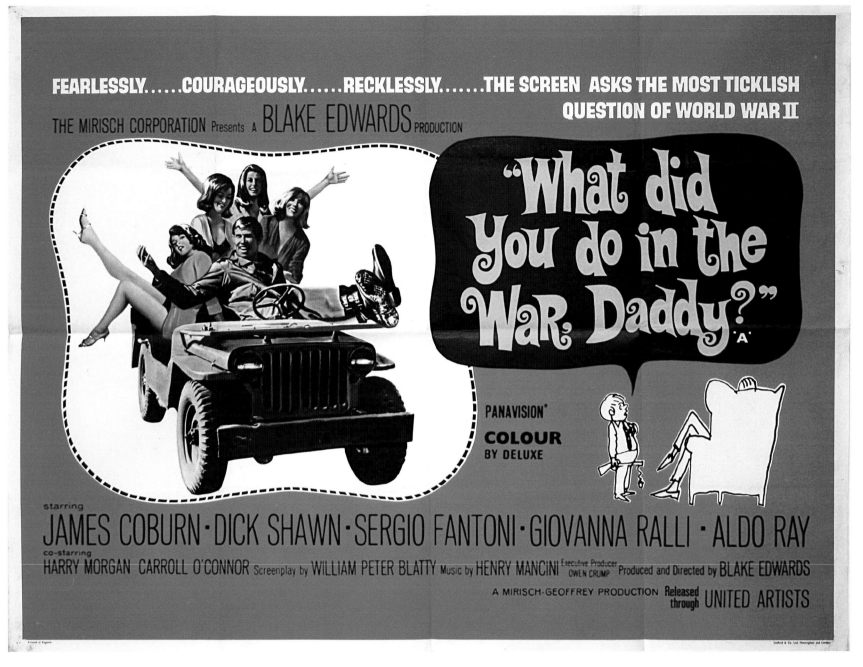

WHAT DID YOU DO IN THE WAR DADDY?

Movie made in the USA in 1966 • Poster: UK • Size: 30x40in (76x102cm) • Rarity rating: 3 • Motor: Willys Jeep
Players: Blake Edwards, James Coburn, Aldo Ray, Harry Morgan, Carroll O'Connor

An everyday tale of war, wine, and football

HELL ON WHEELS

Movie made in the USA in 1967
Poster: USA
Size: 27x41in (69x104cm)
Rarity rating: 3
Motor: Stock Cars
Players: Marty Robbins, John Ashley, Connie Smith

Somehow, Marty Robbins singing "Fly, Butterfly, Fly" doesn't seem to go with the hot heads and heavy feet

MONKEYS GO HOME

Movie made in the USA in 1967 • Poster: UK • Size: 30x40in (76x102cm) • Rarity rating: 2 • Motor: Renault 8
Players: Walt Disney, Maurice Chevalier, Dean Jones, Yvette Mimieux

Not even the beautiful Yvette can prevent three chimps hijacking the movie

SEVEN ARTS PRODUCTIONS PRESENTA

LA PORTA SBARRATA

TECHNICOLOR

W WARNER BROS. - SEVEN ARTS

**GIG YOUNG CAROL LYNLEY
OLIVER REED FLORA ROBSON**

PRODOTTO DA PHILLIP HAZELTON   REGIA DI DAVID GREENE
SCENEGGIATURA DI D. B. LEDROV e NATHANIEL TANCHUCK
UNA PRODUZIONE TROY-SCHEECK   EDIZIONE ITALIANA MCMLXVIII

THE SHUTTERED ROOM

Movie made in the UK in 1967 • Poster: Italy • Size: 26x18in (66x46cm) • Rarity rating: 3 • Motor: Ford Thunderbird • Players: Oliver Reed, Flora Robson, Gig Young, Carol Lynley

Also known as Blood Island. Oliver Reed and Flora Robson provided an interesting contrast

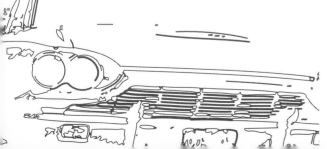

THE WILD REBELS

Movie made in the USA in 1967
Poster: USA
Size: 27x41in (69x104cm)
Rarity rating: 3
Motor: Motorcycles – artist's impression
Players: Steve Alaimo, Willie Pastrano

The artist has made the bikes look about as nutty as fruitcake, but good copy lines and British machines

TRACK OF THUNDER

Movie made in the USA in 1967
Poster: USA
Size: 27x41in (69x104cm)
Rarity rating: 3
Motor: Stock Cars
Players: Tom Kirk, Faith Domergue

Excellent but frustratingly anonymous artwork for this wham bam racing movie

TWO FOR THE ROAD

Movie made in the UK in 1967 • Lobby card: USA • Size: 11x14in (28x36cm) • Rarity rating: 3 • Motor: MG TD
Players: Audrey Hepburn, Albert Finney, Eleanor Bron, Stanley Donen

Finney and Hepburn in a romantic charmer

117

BULLITT

Movie made in the USA in 1968
Poster: France
Size: 47x63in (119x160cm)
Rarity rating: 3
Artist: Landi
Motor: Ford Mustang
Players: Steve McQueen, Jacqueline Bisset, Robert Vaughan

This 2006 French re-release is based on the original Landi artwork, but includes the iconic Mustang, missing from almost all other posters

CHITTY CHITTY BANG BANG

Movie made in the UK in 1968 • Poster: UK • Size: 30x40in (76x102cm) • Rarity rating: 3 • Motor: Chitty Bang Bang • Players: Dick Van Dyke, Louis Zborowski, Sally Ann Howes, Ian Fleming, Lionel Jeffries

Fantasy based on the cars of Count Louis Zborowski. The name of the car allegedly derived from the noise of the driver's fart of fear whilst at the wheel

DANGER DIABOLIK

Movie made in Italy &
France in 1968
Poster: France
Size: 23x30in (58x76cm)
Rarity rating: 4
Artist: Vaissier
Motor: Jaguar
Players: John Philip Law,
Adolfo Celi, Marisa Mell,
Terry-Thomas, Michel Piccoli

Lots of leather, psychedelic
artwork, and an E-Type.
Those were the days ...

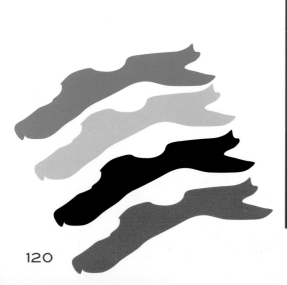

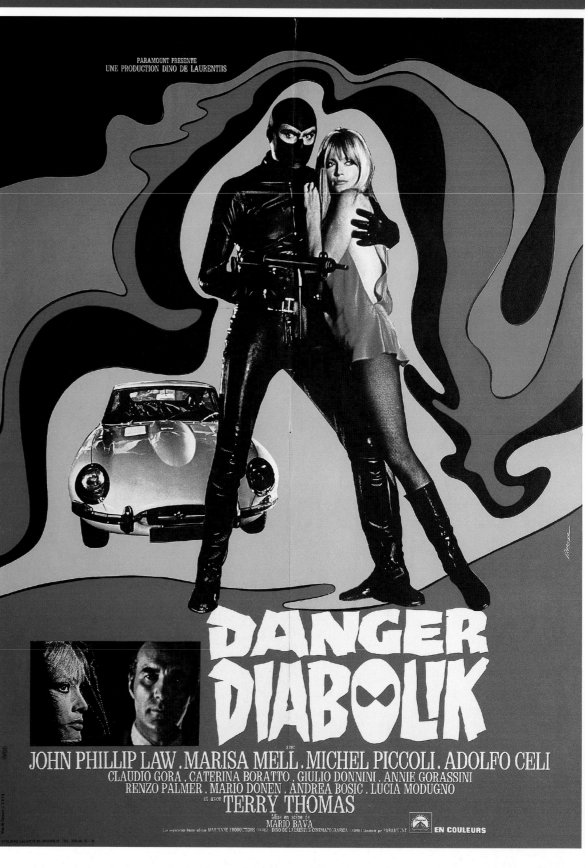

DECLINE AND FALL – OF A BIRDWATCHER

Movie made in the UK in 1968 • Poster: UK • Size: 30x40in (76x102cm) • Rarity rating: 2
Motor: Rolls-Royce • Players: Genevieve Page, Felix Aylmer, Leo McKern, Donald Sinden, Colin Blakely, Donald Wolfit

No wonder the artist's anonymous after his treatment of the headlamp, which is not so much 'Chinese Eye', as "where did I put the microwave" ...

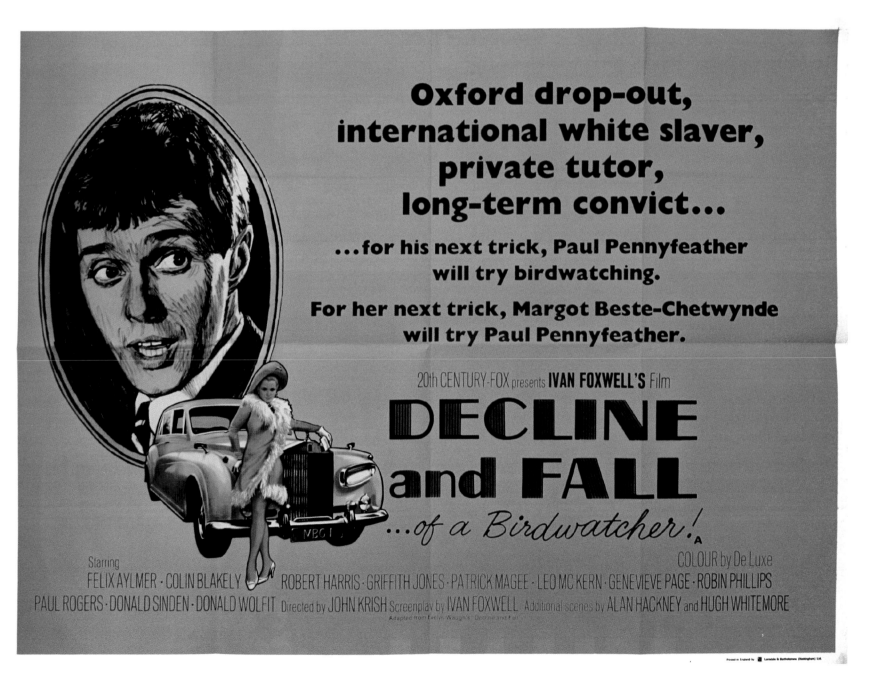

DRIVER

Movie made in the USA in 1968 • Poster: UK • Size: 30x40in (76x102cm) • Rarity rating: 3 • Artist: Bysouth
Motor: Various • Players: Ryan O'Neal, Bruce Dern, Isabelle Adjani

Bold poster: understated movie

GIRL ON A MOTORCYCLE

Movie made in the UK & France in 1968
Poster: France
Size: 23x30in (58x76cm)
Rarity rating: 3
Artist: Vaissier
Motor: Norton 650 motorcycle
Players: Alain Delon, Marianne Faithfull

AKA *La Motocyclette*, and in the US *Naked Under Leather*. Alain Delon and Marianne Faithfull, but not, as many think, on a Harley

EDGAR WALLACE

PARIS - ETOILE FILM presenta

IL TESCHIO DI LONDRA

JOACHIM FUCHSBERGER · SIW MATTSON · CLAUDE FARELL · LIL LINDFORS · PETER MOSBACHER | EASTMANCOLOR
PRODUZIONE RIALTO FILM - PREBEN PHILIPSEN   REGIA: ALFRED VOHRER   ESCLUSIVITA ADAMO FILM | PRIMA EDIZIONE ITALIANA 1968 · ROTOGRAPH · ROMA

IL TESCHIO DI LONDRA

Movie made in Germany in 1968 • Poster: Italy • Size: 26x18in (66x46cm)
Rarity rating: 3 • Motor: Jaguar • Players: Edgar Wallace, Siegfried Rauch

AKA *The Hand of Power* and *The Zombie Walks*. Siegfried Rauch played a British doctor before co-starring in *Le Mans*. The postage stamp above 'Edgar' signifies that 'paper tax' has been paid on this item

KILLICO

Movie made in the USA in 1968
Poster: Italy
Size: 55x39in (140x99cm)
Rarity rating: 4
Artist: Franco
Motor: Grand Prix cars – artist's impression
Players: Fabian, Mimsy Farmer

Better known as *The Wild Racers*. Super poster, with the tyre marks spelling out the names of Grand Prix circuits. Lotus and Cooper models are amongst the artist impressions

LE GANG DU DIMANCHE

Movie made in the USA in 1968
Poster: France
Size: 47x63in (119x160cm)
Rarity rating: 3
Artist: Belinsky
Motor: Citroen DS
Players: Robert Wagner, Mary Tyler Moore, Glynis Johns

AKA *Don't Just Stand There* in the USA

L'HOMME A LA JAGUAR ROUGE

Movie made in Germany in 1968
Poster: France
Size: 47x63in (119x160cm)
Rarity rating: 2
Artist: Saukoff
Motor: Jaguar E-Type
Players: Jerry Cotton, George Nader

George Nader played Jerry Cotton in a string of these cheapies

THE INVINCIBLE SUPERMAN

Movie made in Italy in 1968
Poster: UK
Size: 27x49in (69x124cm)
Rarity rating: 3
Motor: Jaguar, Chevrolet
Players: Guy Madison, Ken Wood

Rare British one sheet with a tacky look that flatters the movie. At least there's an E-Type in there, plus a very strangely equipped Chevy Station Wagon

KEN WOOD · GUY MADISON · LIZ BARRET · DIANA LORIS · PAUL MAXWELL

EASTMANCOLOR

THE THOMAS CROWN AFFAIR

Movie made in the USA in 1968 • Lobby card: France • Size: 11x9in (28x23cm) • Rarity rating: 3
Motor: Beach Buggy • Players: Steve McQueen, Faye Dunaway

Steve McQueen, Faye Dunaway, and a Corvair-engined Buggy

La Compagnie Mirisch présente
Steve McQueen
Faye Dunaway dans

un film de **Norman Jewison**

L'affaire Thomas Crown
(THE THOMAS CROWN AFFAIR)

TECHNICOLOR

Distribué par
Les Artistes Associés

United Artists
Entertainment from
Transamerica Corporation

VISA N° 2998

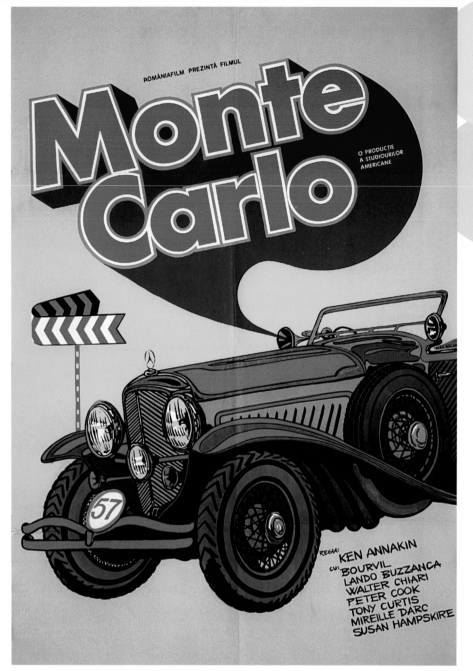

MONTE CARLO OR BUST

Movie made in the UK in 1969 • Poster: Italy • Size: 55x39in (140x99cm) • Rarity rating: 3 • Artist: Ronald Searle • Motor: Caricature

Epic motor racing comedy, called, in the US, *Those Daring Young Men in Their Jaunty Jalopies*. Catchy

MONTE CARLO OR BUST

Movie made in the UK in 1969 • Poster: Romania Size: 38x27in (97x69cm) • Rarity rating: 4 • Artist: Alex Balan • Motor: Mercedes-Benz • Players: Bourvil, Peter Cook, Walter Chiari, Tony Curtis, Gert Frobe, Susan Hampshire, Dudley Moore, Jack Hawkins, Terry-Thomas, Eric Sykes, Ken Annakin, Willy Rushton, Hattie Jacques

Unique and wonderful artwork for this rally romp. Although the car looks more Duesenberg than Mercedes, that three-pointed star on the radiator can't be argued with

THE ITALIAN JOB

Movie made in the UK in 1969
Poster: Italy
Size: 55x39in (140x99cm)
Rarity rating: 4
Motor: Mini-Cooper
Players: Michael Caine, Noel Coward, Benny Hill, Raf Vallone, Rossano Brazzi, Tony Beckley, John Le Mesurier, Maggie Blye, Fred Emney, Irene Handl

The British and Italian posters for this classic movie are head-and-shoulders above the rest

131

THE RACING SCENE

Movie made in the USA in 1969
Poster: USA
Size: 27x41in (69x104cm)
Rarity rating: 3
Motor: Surtees TS5
Players: James Garner

A season in the life of James Garner's racing team

VIRAGES

Movie made in the USA in 1969 • Poster: France
Size: 23x30in (58x76cm) • Rarity rating: 3
Artist: Oussenko • Motor: Gurney Eagle
Players: Paul Newman, Robert Wagner, Joanne
Woodward, Bobby Unser, Dan Gurney

A little artistic licence has been used on the Eagle, but
a great portrait of Paul Newman in the movie known
in the UK and USA as *Winning*

WINNING

Movie made in the USA in 1969 • Poster: UK
Size: 30x40in (76x102cm) • Rarity rating: 3
Motor: Eagle – artist's impression

This Paul Newman film was known as *Indianapolis*
in most of Europe, with the exception of France and
Belgium, where it was entitled *Virages*

AMORE FORMULA 2

Movie made in Italy in 1970
Poster: Italy
Size: 55x39in (140x99cm)
Rarity rating: 3
Artist: Gasparri
Motor: Artist's impression
Players: Giacomo Agostini, Mal

Agony without the ecstasy, but a vibrant poster, nonetheless

BORSALINO

Movie made in France in 1970
Poster: Italy
Size: 55x39in (140x99cm)
Rarity rating: 3
Players: Lorraine Dietrich, Alain
Delon, Jean-Paul Belmondo

French classic with Delon and
Belmondo

BRAD HARRIS · OLINKA BEROVA

FORMULA 1
NELL'INFERNO DEL GRAND PRIX

HANS VON BORSODY - IVANO STACCIOLI
MARIANNE HOFFMANN - LOUIS WILLIAMS
GIANCARLO BAGHETTI E FRANCO RESSEL
E PER LA PRIMA VOLTA SULLO SCHERMO
CON GRAHAM HILL
2 VOLTE CAMPIONE DEL MONDO DI FORMULA 1
GIACOMO AGOSTINI

UNA PRODUZIONE N.C. · DISTRIBUZIONE DIFI   REGIA JAMES REED

EASTMANCOLOR - CROMOSCOPE

FORMULA ONE, NELL'INFERNO DEL GRAND PRIX

Movie made in Italy in 1970 • Poster: Italy • Size: 25x18in (64x46cm) • Rarity rating: 3 • Motor: Lotus Cosworth
Players: Giacomo Agostini, Graham Hill, Giancarlo Baghetti

The red car appears to be based on the Lotus 49 Cosworth. Excellent moody portrait of Graham Hill and 'Ago'

136

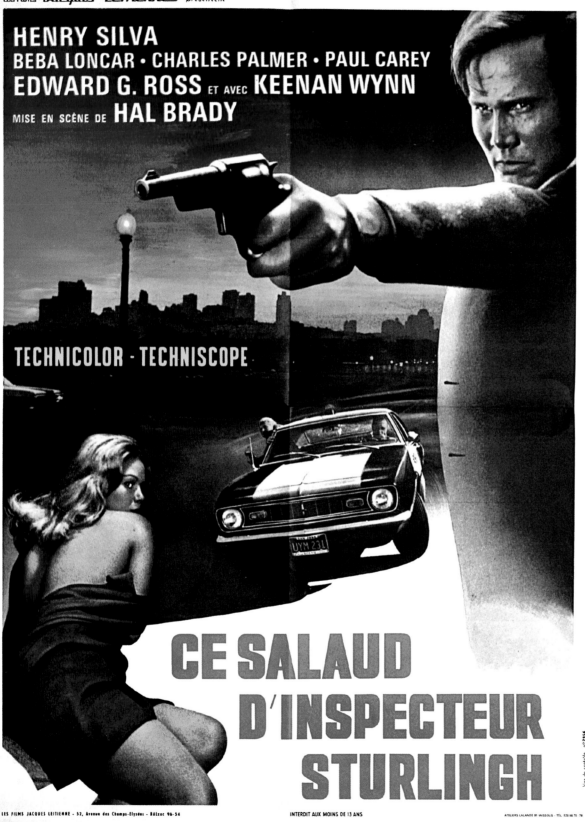

FRAME UP

Movie made in Italy in 1970
Poster: France
Size: 23x30in (58x76cm)
Rarity rating: 3
Artist: Lalande
Motor: Chevrolet Camaro
– artist's impression
Players: Henry Silva, Keenan Wynn

AKA *The Falling Man* in the USA

GOLDFINGER

Movie made in the UK in 1970
Poster: Japan
Size: 20x29in (51x74cm)
Rarity rating: 4
Motor: Aston Martin, Ford
Players: Sean Connery, Ian Fleming,
Honor Blackman, Gert Frobe,
Shirley Eaton, Harold Sakata,
Bernard Lee, Lois Maxwell, Cec
Linder

This 1970 re-release poster has
more appeal than the first release,
featuring the DB5 and a Mustang

THE CHALLENGERS

Movie made in the USA in 1970
Poster: Italy
Size: 55x39in (140x99cm)
Rarity rating: 3
Artist: Franco
Motor: Formula One cars – artist's impression
Players: Darren McGavin, Sean Garrison, Nico Minardos

Brilliant artwork for what began life in 1969 as the first TV movie commissioned by CBS

TRAFFIC

Movie made in France in 1970 • Poster: Italy • Size: 26x18in (66x46cm) • Rarity rating: 3 • Motor: Citroen • Players: Jacques Tati

M Hulot, once again in the hands of Jacques Tati. You can see the shadow of the mechanism required to tilt the DS, under the car

140

DUEL

Movie made in the USA in 1971
Poster: France
Size: 47x63in (119x160cm)
Rarity rating: 2
Artist: Landi
Motor: Big rig
Players: Steven Spielberg, Dennis Weaver

Spielberg's first biggie

141

EURO INTERNATIONAL FILMS PRESENTA

GIAN MARIA VOLONTE' IN

LA CLASSE OPERAIA VA IN PARADISO

CON MARIANGELA MELATO • GINO PERNICE • LUIGI DIBERTI • DONATO CASTELLANETA • E CON SALVO RANDONE • UN FILM DI ELIO PETRI • PRODOTTO DALLA EURO INTERNATIONAL FILMS S.p.A. • SOGGETTO E SCENEGGIATURA DI ELIO PETRI – UGO PIRRO • PRODUTTORE ESECUTIVO UGO TUCCI

EASTMANCOLOR DELLA SPES – SCHERMO PANORAMICO

LA CLASSE OPERAIA VA IN PARADISO

Movie made in Italy in 1971 • Poster: Italy • Size: 18x26in (46x66cm) • Rarity rating: 3
Motor: Citroen • Players: Gian Maria Volonte

Also known as *LuLu The Tool*, and *The Working Class Goes To Heaven*. The Citroen DS (or ID) is a favourite on European posters

LE MANS

Movie made in the USA in 1971 • Poster: France • Size: 47x63in (119x160cm) • Rarity rating: 4 • Artist: Ferracci • Motor: Porsche 917 • Players: Steve McQueen, Siegfried Rauch, Elga Andersen, Ronald Leigh-Hunt

Probably the best of all the *Le Mans* posters, with the cars and the fine McQueen portrait

LE MANS

Movie made in the USA in 1971 • Poster: Italy • Size: 79x54in (201x137cm) • Rarity rating: 4 • Motor: Ferrari, Alfa Romeo, Porsche

Pretty much a mirror image of the French poster, but, being Italian, the emphasis is on Ferrari, rather than the Porsche 917 that features in most material

LE MANS

Movie made in the USA in 1971 • Poster: Czechoslovakia 1973 Size: 16x11in (41x28cm) Rarity rating: 3 Artist: Ziegler Motor: Porsche 917

This Czech offering is one of the most effective of all the *Le Mans* posters

SUDDEN TERROR

Movie made in the UK in 1971
Poster: USA
Size: 27x41in (69x104cm)
Rarity rating: 2
Motor: Triumph Herald
Players: Mark Lester, Susan George, Lionel Jeffries, Jeremy Kemp, Peter Vaughan

A very rare poster outing for the Herald. In the UK the movie was known as *Eye Witness*

THE LAST RUN

They told him it was just a driving job.

They didn't tell him seven killers would be waiting at the end of the road.

MGM Presents

GEORGE C. SCOTT
"THE LAST RUN"

Co-starring

TONY MUSANTE · TRISH VAN DEVERE

Original Screenplay by ALAN SHARP · Produced by CARTER DE HAVEN · Directed by

RICHARD FLEISCHER · Music by JERRY GOLDSMITH · METROCOLOR · PANAVISION® MGM

Movie made in the USA in 1971
Poster: USA
Size: 27x41in (69x104cm)
Rarity rating: 2
Motor: BMW 503
Players: George C Scott, Tony Musante, Trish Van Devere

The charismatic George C Scott, with an even more charismatic BMW

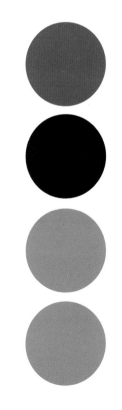

TWO LANE BLACKTOP

Movie made in the USA in 1971
• Poster: Japan • Size: 20x29in (51x74cm)
Rarity rating: 4 • Motor: Pontiac GTO
Players: James Taylor, Warren Oates

Stark poster for this dark cult movie

TWO LANE BLACKTOP

Movie made in the USA in 1971
Poster: USA • Size: 27x41in (69x104cm)
Rarity rating: 4 • Motor: Chevrolet Belair
Players: Warren Oates, James Taylor, Laurie
Bird, Dennis Wilson

Good portraits of Warren Oates and James
Taylor, with the GTO – rather than the Chevy
– featuring

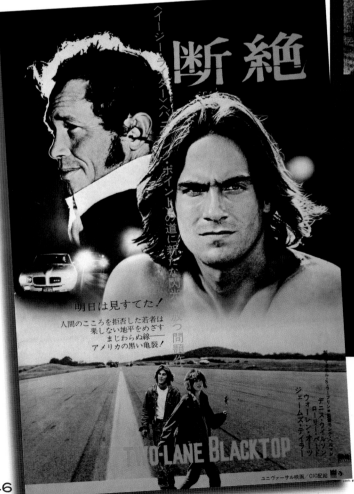

JAMES TAYLOR IS THE DRIVER
WARREN OATES IS GTO
LAURIE BIRD IS THE GIRL
DENNIS WILSON IS THE MECHANIC

TWO-LANE BLACKTOP
IS THE PICTURE

TWO-LANE BLACK-TOP

JAMES TAYLOR · WARREN OATES · LAURIE BIRD · DENNIS WILSON
Screenplay by RUDOLPH WURLITZER and WILL CORRY · Story by WILL CORRY · Directed by MONTE HELLMAN · Produced by MICHAEL S. LAUGHLIN
A MICHAEL S. LAUGHLIN PRODUCTION · A UNIVERSAL PICTURE · TECHNICOLOR® · R

VANISHING POINT

Movie made in the USA in 1971 • Poster: UK • Size: 30x40in (76x102cm) • Rarity rating: 4 • Artist: Tom Chantrell
Motor: Dodge, Jaguar • Players: Barry Newman, Cleavon Little, Dean Jagger

One of the greats. Chantrell makes terrific use of the Challenger, and the copy line is inspired

VANISHING POINT

Movie made in the USA in 1971 • Poster: France • Size: 47x63in (119x160cm) • Rarity rating: 3 • Artist: Ferracci • Motor: Dodge Challenger

Another great design by Ferracci, which accentuates the hunted, haunted eyes of Barry Newman

ON ANY SUNDAY

Movie made in the USA in 1972
• Poster: USA • Size: 27x41in (69x104cm)
• Rarity rating: 4 • Motor: Motorbikes •
Players: Steve McQueen, Bruce Brown

Director, Bruce Brown, made the surfing classic *Endless Summer*. What this poster doesn't say about this movie is that the main attraction is Steve McQueen having a rowdy day out with his mates

ON ANY SUNDAY

Movie made in the USA in 1972 • Poster: Italy
Size: 55x39in (140x99cm) • Rarity rating: 4
Motor: Motorbikes

McQueen and chums having a ball

PORNO- MOTEL

Movie made in the USA in 1972 • Poster: Germany • Size: 23x33in (58x84cm)
Rarity rating: 3 • Motor: Ford Mustang • Players: Vic Lance, Christine Mathis

AKA *Weekend Lovers* in the USA

WEEKEND OF A CHAMPION

Movie made in the UK in 1972
Poster: Germany
Size: 23x33in (58x84cm)
Rarity rating: 4
Artist: Krajewski
Motor: Tyrrell F1
Players: Jackie Stewart, Roman Polanski

Polanski's documentary on Jackie and Helen Stewart at the 1971 Monaco GP. AKA *Afternoon of a Champion* in the USA

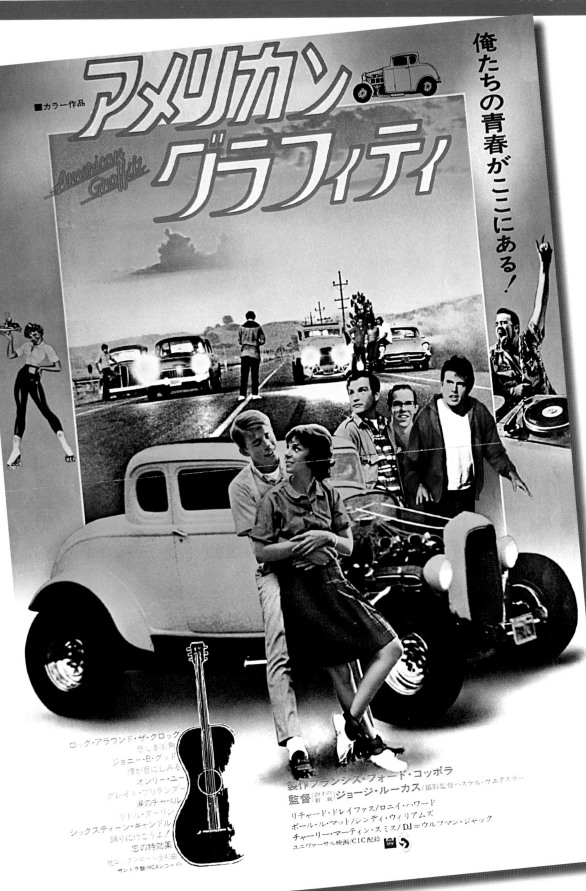

AMERICAN GRAFFITI

Movie made in the USA in 1973
Poster: Japan
Size: 20x29in (51x74cm)
Rarity rating: 3
Motor: Ford Hot Rod, Chevrolet
Players: Richard Dreyfus, Ron Howard, Wolfman Jack, Bo Hopkins, Paul Le Mat, Charles Martin Smith, Cindy Williams, Candy Clark

Probably the most coveted poster for this cult movie. The Chevy Belair was also used in *Two Lane Blacktop*

HEAVY TRAFFIC

Movie made in the USA in 1973
Poster: Germany
Size: 23x33in (58x84cm)
Rarity rating: 2
Artist: Ralph Bakshi
Motor: Unknown
Players: Ralph Bakshi

Paricularly robust poster for the German release of this mostly animated grotesque

IL DIAVOLO DEL VOLANTE

Movie made in the USA in 1973
Poster: Italy
Size: 55x39in (140x99cm)
Rarity rating: 3
Motor: Race car – artist's impression
Players: Junior Johnson, Jeff Bridges, Valerie Perrine

Odd that this poster for *Last American Hero*, the Jr Johnson story, features open-wheelers. You can almost hear the Italian distributor saying "Let's make it as much like a Ferrari as possible"

PIGALLE: CARREFOUR DES ILLUSIONS

Movie made in France in 1973
Poster: France
Size: 47x63in (119x160cm)
Rarity rating: 3
Motor: Citroen DS
Players: Evelyne Scott, Jean-Michel Dhermay, Beatrice Constantini

Every seedy facet of Paris features in this brilliantly executed poster, whose artist is as anonymous as the film itself

SUMMERTIME KILLER

Movie made in Spain in 1973 • Poster: UK • Size: 30x40in (76x102cm) • Rarity rating: 3 • Motor: Porsche 911
Players: Karl Malden, Olivia Hussey, Christopher Mitchum, Raf Vallone

Violent Euro-flick with US actors, made in Spain in 1972 as *Un Verano Para Matar*

Columbia Pictures presents

Robert Shaw **Sarah Miles** in

The Hireling A

with

Peter Egan · Caroline Mortimer
Elizabeth Sellars

Screenplay by Wolf Mankowitz · Executive Producer Terence Baker
Produced by Ben Arbeid · Directed by Alan Bridges
A World Film Services Production

 RELEASED BY COLUMBIA PICTURES (DISTRIBUTION) LTD

GRAND PRIZE
WINNER
CANNES FILM
FESTIVAL

THE HIRELING

Movie made in the UK in 1973 • Poster: UK • Size: 30x40in (76x102cm)
Rarity rating: 2 • Artist: Vic Fair • Motor: Rolls-Royce • Players: Robert Shaw, Sarah
Miles, Peter Egan, Wolf Mankowitz

Beautiful and imaginative design and artwork from Mr Fair

FUNNY CAR SUMMER

Movie made in the USA in 1974
Poster: USA
Size: 27x41in (69x104cm)
Rarity rating: 2
Artist: Glen Edwards
Motor: Dragsters
Players: Jim Dunn

Features various forms of drag-racing and described by one responsible source as a "wretched waste of celluloid". Better rush right out and get a copy ...

GONE IN 60 Seconds

Movie made in the USA in 1974
Poster: UK
Size: 30x40in (76x102cm)
Rarity rating: 3
Motor: Ford Mustang
Players: H B Halicki, Marion Busia, George Cole, Parnelli Jones, J C Agajanian

The best poster of the original version, starring Eleanor

GONE IN 60 SECONDS

Movie made in the USA in 1974
Lobby card: Germany
Size: 9x11in (23x28cm)
Rarity rating: 3
Motor: Ford Mustang

Eleanor takes a pounding in this German lobby card

ROGER MOORE TONY CURTIS

MONTEKARLO HAREKÂTI

SUSAN GEORGE

harun film

RENKLİ TÜRKÇE Yönetmen ROY WARD BAKER

MISSION: MONTE CARLO

Movie made in the UK in 1974
Poster: Turkey
Size: 27x39in (69x99cm)
Rarity rating: 3
Motor: Formula One Racers
Players: Tony Curtis, Roger Moore,
Susan George

Not so much a movie as two
episodes of *The Persuaders*,
chopped about a bit

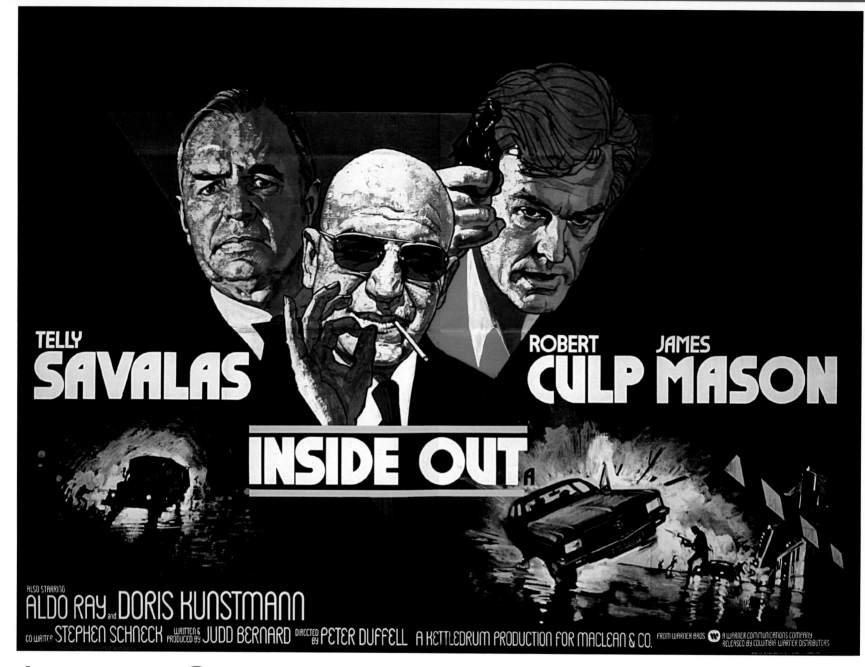

TELLY **SAVALAS** ROBERT **CULP** JAMES **MASON**

INSIDE OUT

ALSO STARRING **ALDO RAY** AND **DORIS KUNSTMANN**
CO-WRITER STEPHEN SCHNECK WRITTEN & PRODUCED BY JUDD BERNARD DIRECTED BY PETER DUFFELL A KETTLEDRUM PRODUCTION FOR MACLEAN & CO. FROM WARNER BROS A WARNER COMMUNICATIONS COMPANY RELEASED BY COLUMBIA WARNER DISTRIBUTORS

INSIDE OUT

Movie made in the UK in 1975 • Poster: UK • Size: 30x40in (76x102cm) • Rarity rating: 3 • Motor: Opel
Players: Telly Savalas, James Mason, Robert Culp

Anglo-German production, with highly effective poster

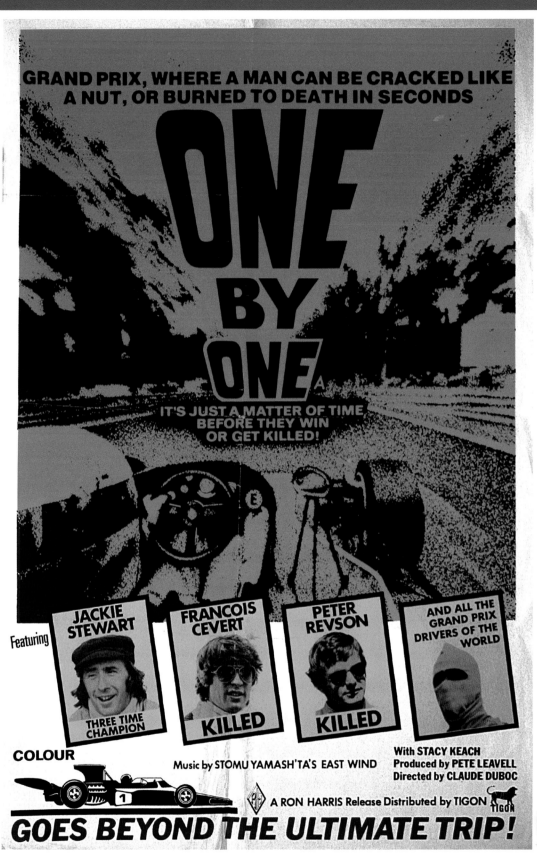

ONE BY ONE

Movie made in the USA in 1975
Poster: UK
Size: 30x20in (76x51cm)
Rarity rating: 3
Motor: Formula One motorsport
Players: Jackie Stewart, Francois Cevert, Peter Revson

Sensationalised documentary about F1

LE BON ET LES MECHANTS

Movie made in France in 1976
Poster: France
Size: 23x30in (58x76cm)
Rarity rating: 2
Artist: Ferracci
Motor: Citroen Traction
Players: Claude Lelouch, Marlene Jobert, Jacques Dutronc, Bruno Cremer, Brigitte Fossey, Jacques Villeret

AKA *The Good Guys and the Bad Guys*

162

LES VÉCÉS ÉTAIENT FERMÉS DE L'INTÉRIEUR

Movie made in France in 1976
Poster: France
Size: 23x30in (58x76cm)
Rarity rating: 3
Artist: Sole
Motor: Citroen Traction
Players: Coluche, Rochefort, Patrice Leconte

A movie that was either a biting satire of French cop movies. or clumsy mysoginist tripe, depending on your point of view

MADO

Movie made in France in 1976
Poster: France
Size: 23x30in (58x76cm)
Rarity rating: 2
Artist: Ferracci
Motor: Citroen DS
Players: Michel Piccoli, Romy Schneider, Jacques Dutronc, Ottavia Piccolo

Unfortunately for Romy fanciers, she appears for a very short part of this rather long movie

SAFARI EXPRESS

Movie made in Italy in 1976
Poster: Italy
Size: 55x39in (140x99cm)
Rarity rating: 2
Motor: Landrover
Players: Ursula Andress, Jack Palance, Biba

Ursula Andress, Jack Palance, a Landrover, a Dakota and a chimp; something for everyone

Martine BRETON-GIRARD présente

ALICE CONSTANT

un film de

CHRISTINE LAURENT

avec

AGNÈS LAURENT

AGNÈS DE BRUNHOFF

ANTOINE BOURSEILLER

ANDRÉE TAINSY

Image: RENATO BERTA · Son: RICHARD ZOLFO · Montage: FRANÇOISE BELLOUX

Co-production: Z Productions · Institut National de l'Audiovisuel · SERDDAV · EITSON (Paris) Film Kollektiv (Zurich) · Janus Film · Distribution: HELENE FILMS

ALICE CONSTANT

Movie made in France in 1977
Poster: France
Size: 47x63in (119x160cm)
Rarity rating: 3
Motor: Peugeot 203
Players: Christine Laurent, Agnes Laurent

Charming poster design for this movie, which is little known, even in France

CRUISIN' HIGH

Movie made in the USA in 1977
Poster: USA
Size: 27x41in (69x104cm)
Rarity rating: 2
Motor: Chevrolet
Players: David Kyle

Movie originally made in '76 as *Cat Murkil and the Silks*. Apparently, the Belair stole the show ...

LA NUIT DE SAINT GERMAIN DES PRÉS

Movie made in France in1977
Poster: France
Size: 47x63in (119x160cm)
Rarity rating: 2
Artist: Milet
Motor: Peugeot 202, Voisin
Players: Michel Galabru, Mort Shuman

Crime story based on the Leo Malet novel. Lovely dark, yet glitzy, poster art

SPEEDTRAP

Movie made in the USA in 1977
Poster: USA
Size: 27x41in (69x104cm)
Rarity rating: 2
Motor: Jensen Interceptor
Players: Joe Don Baker, Tyne Daly

Super artwork with portraits of Tyne Daly and Joe Don Baker, and a pretty faithful likeness of the Jensen

THE CAR

Movie made in the USA in 1977
Poster: France
Size: 47x63in (119x160cm)
Rarity rating: 3
Artist: Mouth
Motor: Lincoln
Players: James Brolin, Kathleen Lloyd, John Marley

A unique take on *Enfer Mecanique*

170

THE FJ HOLDEN

Movie made in Australia in 1977
Poster: Australia
Size: 27x40in (69x102cm)
Rarity rating: 3
Motor: Holden
Players: Paul Couzens, Eva Dickinson

Classic Oz culture. The offensive language warning near the bottom of the poster seems to be stating the obvious ...

FORMULA ONE: SPEED FEVER

Movie made in Italy in 1978
Poster: Australia
Size: 27x40in (69x102cm)
Rarity rating: 3
Motor: Formula One Racer
Players: Mario Andretti, Niki Lauda, Stirling Moss, Jody Scheckter, James Hunt, Emerson Fittipaldi, Colin Chapman, Jackie Ickyx, Clay Regazzoni

A documentary with a vast cast of actors and drivers, advertised in this particularly lurid fashion

HOOPER

Movie made in the USA in 1978 • Poster: UK • Size: 30x40in (76x102cm) • Rarity rating: 2 • Artist: Bysouth
Motor: Pontiac Firebird Trans-Am • Players: Burt Reynolds, Jan-Michael Vincent, Sally Field, Brian Keith

The rocket jump captured beautifully, and with faithful attention to the Pontiac, by Brian Bysouth

MILOSNE ZYCIE BUDIMIRA TRAJKOVICIA

Movie made in Yugoslavia in 1978
Poster: Poland
Size: 19x26in (48x66cm)
Rarity rating: 3
Artist: Zbikowski
Motor: Hooterhauler
Players: Milena Dravic, Mica Tomic

A romantic comedy: who said romance was dead?

SENZA RAGIONE

Movie made in Italy in 1978
Poster: Italy
Size: 55x39in (140x99cm)
Rarity rating: 3
Motor: Alfa Romeo Giulia
Players: Telly Savalas, Franco Nero, Mark Lester

Known in the USA as *Redneck*

FAST COMPANY

Movie made in the USA in 1979
Poster: Turkey
Size: 27x40in (69x102cm)
Rarity rating: 2
Motor: Ferrari
Players: Jody Scheckter, David Cronenberg, William Smith, John Saxon, Claudia Jennings, Judy Foster

Here's a movie that was regarded as a drag-racing classic, but the Turkish distributor appears to have got hold of the wrong end of the stick. At the top is Jody Scheckter on his way to winning the F1 World Championship in 1979. Apart from the Ferrari there appears to be a totalled John Player Lotus, a Tyrrell, Renault and McLaren. Not a funny-car in sight (except perhaps the Lotus that year)

VAN NUYS BOULEVARD

Movie made in the USA in 1979
Poster: USA
Size: 27x41in (69x104cm)
Rarity rating: 2
Motor: Ford Hot Rod
Players: Bill Adler, Cynthia Wood

Small-town boy hits California;
California hits back

GEORGE AND MILDRED

Movie made in the UK in 1980 • Poster: UK • Size: 30x40in (76x102cm) • Rarity rating: 3 • Artist: Tom Beauvais
Motor: Morris Minor 1000
Yootha Joyce, Brian Murphy, Stratford Johns

Lovely caricature of the Minor Convertible

She's still trying to steer him towards romance– He still doesn't know what she's driving at.

JACK GILL Presents for CHIPS PRODUCTIONS
A CINEMA ARTS INTERNATIONAL PRODUCTION
YOOTHA JOYCE BRIAN MURPHY in
GEORGE AND MILDRED A
Also Starring STRATFORD JOHNS
NORMAN ESHLEY SHEILA FEARN
KENNETH COPE DAVID BARRY
Based on characters created by
BRIAN COOKE and JOHNNIE MORTIMER
Screenplay by DICK SHARPLES Executive Producer BRIAN LAWRENCE
Produced by ROY SKEGGS Directed by PETER FRAZER-JONES
Released by ITC FILM DISTRIBUTORS LTD

HERBIE GOES BANANAS

Movie made in the USA in 1980 • Poster: UK • Size: 30x40in
(76x102cm) • Rarity rating: 2 • Motor: Volkswagen
Players: Cloris Leachman, Walt Disney, Charles Martin-Smith,
John Vernon, Harvey Korman

A total of 26 Beetles were used in the making of this film. Could
be that Beetles and bulls don't mix

HERBIE GOES TO MONTE CARLO

Movie made in the USA in 1977 • Poster: France
Size: 63x23in (160x58cm) • Rarity rating: 2
Motor: Volkswagen Beetle, Lancia Monte Carlo
Players: Dean Jones, Don Knotts, Julie Sommars, Roy Kinnear

Unusual poster size, known as a 'pantalon', indicates that this
may be a 1980s re-release

179

RALLYE

Movie made in Russia in 1980
Poster: Russia
Size: 11x16in (28x41cm)
Rarity rating: 3
Motor: Porsche
Players: Aloiz Brenc

Obscure documentary, but lovely
poster for the 911

RALLYE

Sovětský film / Kriminální příběh z prostředí
mezinárodních automobilových závodů
Režie: Aloiz Brenč / Hrají: Vitautas Tomkus,
Roland Zagorskij, Valentina Titovová aj.

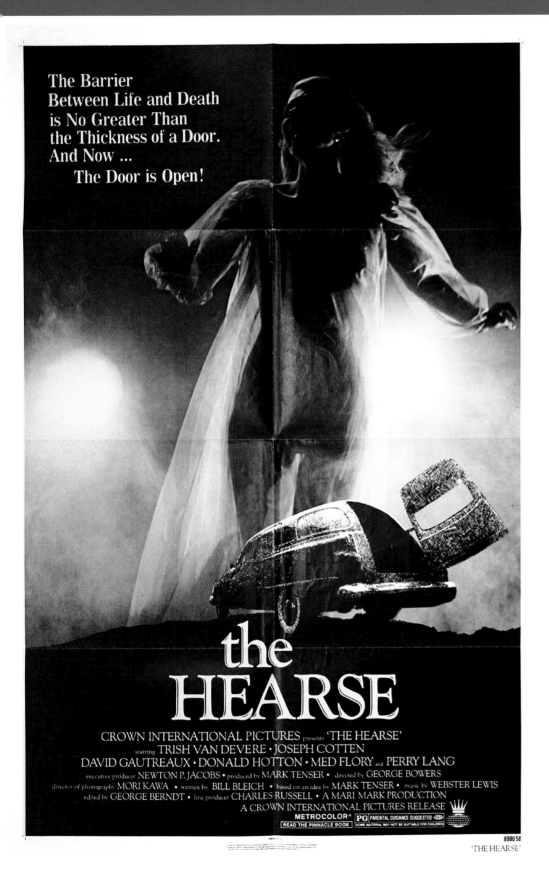

RIP

THE HEARSE

Movie made in the USA in 1980
Poster: USA
Size: 27x41in (69x104cm)
Rarity rating: 2
Motor: Cadillac Hearse
Players: Trish Van Devere, Joseph Cotton

The perfect eerie artwork for this supernatural B-movie

WYROK SMIERCI

Movie made in Poland in 1980 • Poster: Poland • Size: 26x38in (66x97cm) • Rarity rating: 4
Motor: Mercedes-Benz • Players: Wojciech Wysocki, Doris Kunstmann, Jerzy Bonczak

Most probably a late 1930s 170v Mercedes-Benz on this ultra-rare poster for a spy thriller set in 1943

DIVA

Here comes a new kind of French New Wave.

Movie made in France in 1981
Poster: USA
Size: 27x41in (69x104cm)
Rarity rating: 3
Motor: Studebaker
Players: Richard Bohringer, Jean-Jacques Beineix, Frederic Andrei, Roland Bertin, Wilhelmenia Wiggins Fernandez

But why the Studebaker, when the film's automotive star was a Citroen Traction?

FANGIO: A LIFE AT 300KPH

Movie made in the UK in 1981
Poster: Italy • Size: 18x26in (46x66cm)
Rarity rating: 4 • Motor: Ferrari

Juan Manuel Fangio in the Ferrari at Monaco. This film had a very limited release

FANGIO: A LIFE AT 300KPH

Movie made in the UK in 1981
Poster: Italy
Size: 55x39in (140x99cm)
Rarity rating: 4 • Artist: Giniello
Motor: Maserati 250F
Players: Hugh Hudson, Juan Manuel Fangio

Splendid poster for Hugh Hudson's little-seen bio-pic

FOR YOUR EYES ONLY

Movie made in the UK and
USA in 1981
Poster: France
Size: 47x63in (119x160cm)
Rarity rating: 2
Artist: Bill Gold
Motor: Lotus, Citroen
Players: Roger Moore,
Carole Bouquet, Topol,
Lynn-Holly Johnson, Julian
Glover

One of the most famous
images in movies. The
buttocks had varying
degrees of cover,
dependent on the country
it was intended for

ALBERT R. BROCCOLI présente

ROGER MOORE

dans le rôle de

JAMES BOND 007

d'après l'œuvre de IAN FLEMING

RIEN QUE POUR VOS YEUX

(FOR YOUR EYES ONLY)

avec CAROLE BOUQUET · TOPOL · LYNN-HOLLY JOHNSON · JULIAN GLOVER

Produit par ALBERT R. BROCCOLI   Réalisé par JOHN GLEN

Scénario de RICHARD MAIBAUM et MICHAEL G. WILSON   Producteur Exécutif MICHAEL G. WILSON

Musique de BILL CONTI   Décors créés par PETER LAMONT

Producteur Associé TOM PEVSNER   PANAVISION   TECHNICOLOR

BANDE SONORE ORIGINALE DU FILM
SUR DISQUES ET CASSETTES LIBERTY

Chanson du générique interprétée par SHEENA EASTON

185

GOODBYE

Movie made in New Zealand
in 1981
Poster: Pakistan
Size: 28x39in (71x99cm)
Rarity rating: 4
Artist: Afzal Studio
Motor: Austin Mini
Players: Tony Barry, Kelly Johnson, Shirley Gruar, Clare Oberman

Kiwi road movie, originally entitled *Goodbye Pork Pie*; changed in Pakistan for obvious reasons. Strap line on UK poster was "They hit the road, and the road hit back"

THE PINCHCLIFFE GRAND PRIX

Movie made in Norway in 1975;
released 1981
Poster: USA
Size: 27x41in (69x104cm)
Rarity rating: 2
Artist: Joe Smith
Motor: Il Tempo Gigante
Players: Ivo Caprino

This was a beautiful work of 'stop animation'. The car still exists, fully working and to full scale

THE JUNKMAN

Movie made in the USA in 1982
Poster: USA
Size: 27x41in (69x104cm)
Rarity rating: 4
Motor: Chevrolet Corvette
Players: H B Halicki, Christopher Stone, Susan Shaw, Lang Jeffries, Hoyt Axton, George Barris

Rough-and-ready follow-up to Halicki's *Gone in 60 Seconds*

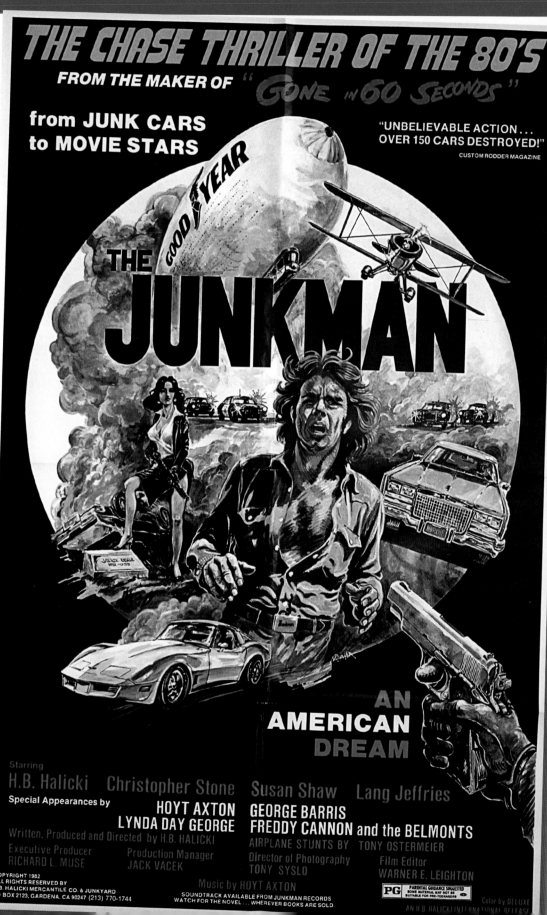

CHRISTINE

Movie made in the USA in 1983 • Poster: UK • Size: 30x40in (76x102cm) • Rarity rating: 2 • Motor: Plymouth Fury
Players: John Carpenter, Keith Gordon, John Stockwell, Alexandra Paul, Robert Prosky, Harry Dean Stanton

Superb poster design conveys the evil essence of Stephen King's nightmare motor

LA LUNE DANS LE CANIVEA

Movie made in France in 1983
Poster: France
Size: 47x63in (119x160cm)
Rarity rating: 2
Artist: Mascii
Motor: Ferrari
Players: Gerard Depardieu, Natassja Kinski, Jean-Jacques Beineix

A 275 GTB, allowing the artist a little leeway. The movie was known in the US as *The Moon in the Gutter*

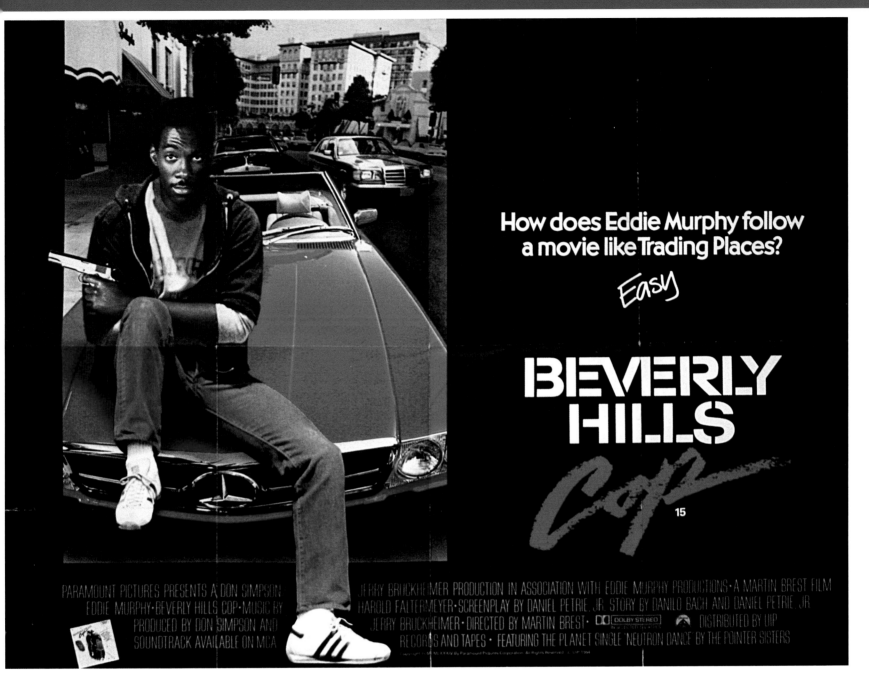

How does Eddie Murphy follow
a movie like Trading Places?

Easy

BEVERLY HILLS COP

15

PARAMOUNT PICTURES PRESENTS A DON SIMPSON
EDDIE MURPHY·BEVERLY HILLS COP·MUSIC BY
PRODUCED BY DON SIMPSON AND
SOUNDTRACK AVAILABLE ON MCA

JERRY BRUCKHEIMER PRODUCTION IN ASSOCIATION WITH EDDIE MURPHY PRODUCTIONS·A MARTIN BREST FILM
HAROLD FALTERMEYER·SCREENPLAY BY DANIEL PETRIE, JR. STORY BY DANILO BACH AND DANIEL PETRIE, JR
JERRY BRUCKHEIMER·DIRECTED BY MARTIN BREST· DOLBY STEREO DISTRIBUTED BY UIP
RECORDS AND TAPES · FEATURING THE PLANET SINGLE 'NEUTRON DANCE' BY THE POINTER SISTERS

BEVERLY HILLS COP

Movie made in the USA in 1984 • Poster: UK • Size: 30x40in (76x102cm) • Rarity rating: 2 • Motor: Mercedes-Benz SL • Players: Eddie Murphy, Judge Reinhold, Lisa Eilbacher, John Ashton, Ronny Cox, Steven Berkoff

Tailor-made for Eddie Murphy? Nope; the part was originally intended for Sly Stallone

GIACOMO PEZZALI *presenta*
CLAUDIA CARDINALE
un film di PASQUALE SQUITIERI

Claretta

CLARETTA

Movie made in Italy in 1984 • Poster: Italy • Size: 26x18in (66x46cm) • Rarity rating: 2 • Motor: Alfa Romeo
Players: Claudia Cardinale, Gemma Giuliano, Spaak Catherine

Claudia Cardinale stars in the story of Mussolini's mistress

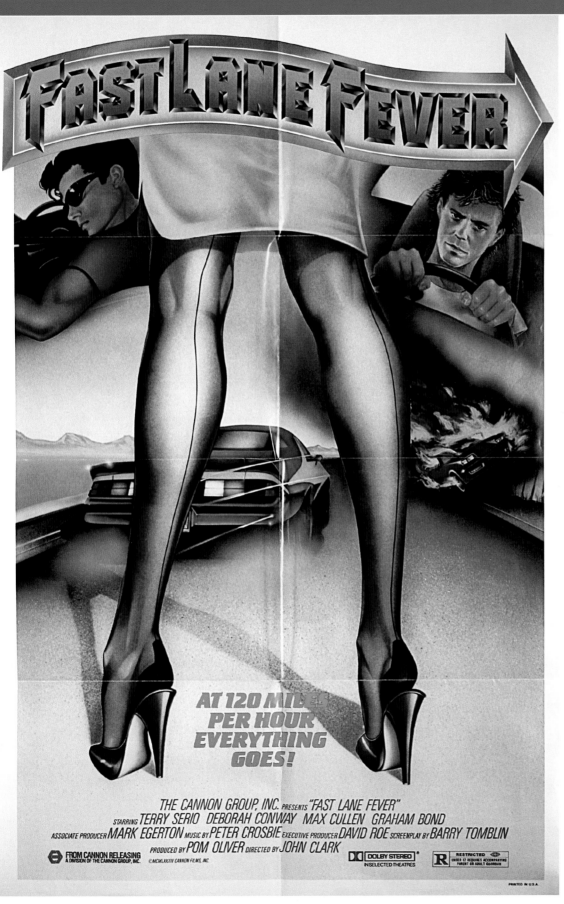

FAST LANE FEVER

Movie made in Australia in
1984
Poster: USA
Size: 27x41in (69x104cm)
Rarity rating: 2
Motor: Artist's impression
Players: Terry Serrio,
Deborah Conway, Max
Cullen, Graham Bond

The car in the movie with
this colour scheme was
a Dodge Challenger;
this looks more like the
well-known Artistic License.
AKA *Running On Empty*.
Recognise the legs?

JOHNNY DANGEROUSLY

Movie made in the USA in 1984 • Poster: UK • Size: 30x40in (76x102cm) • Rarity rating: 2 • Motor: Packard – artist's impression • Players: Michael Keaton, Joe Piscopo, Marilu Henner, Dom DeLuise, Danny DeVito

The movie was universally panned, so it must be worth watching out for

LUI E' PEGGIO DI ME

Movie made in Italy in 1984
Poster: Italy
Size: 55x39in (140x99cm)
Rarity rating: 2
Motor: Morgan
Players: Adriano Celentano, Renato Pozzetto

There are those legs again, this time with an excellent likeness of a 'flat-rad' Morgan

Steven Spielberg przedstawia film science fiction Powrót do przyszłości

reżyseria: Robert Zemeckis
obsada: Christopher Lloyd,
Michael J. Fox, Lea Thompson
Produkcja: USA

He's the only kid ever to get into trouble before he was born.

STEVEN SPIELBERG Presents

BACK TO THE FUTURE PG

A ROBERT ZEMECKIS Film

"BACK TO THE FUTURE" Starring MICHAEL J. FOX
CHRISTOPHER LLOYD · LEA THOMPSON · CRISPIN GLOVER
Written by ROBERT ZEMECKIS & BOB GALE
Music by ALAN SILVESTRI
Produced by BOB GALE and NEIL CANTON
Executive Producers STEVEN SPIELBERG
KATHLEEN KENNEDY and FRANK MARSHALL
Directed by ROBERT ZEMECKIS

Distributed by UIP A UNIVERSAL Picture
© 1985 Universal City Studios, Inc. © UIP 1985
Read the CORGI Paperback and Storybook
Soundtrack Available on MCA Records and Cassettes
Featuring the hit single "The Power of Love" performed by Huey Lewis and the News

BACK TO THE FUTURE

Movie made in the USA in 1985 • Poster: Poland • Size: 26x39in (66x99cm) • Rarity rating: 3 • Artist: Wasilewski • Motor: Artist's impression • Players: Steven Spielberg, Christopher Lloyd, Michael J Fox

OK, it's not much like a DeLorean, but what a superb image from a Polish Master

BACK TO THE FUTURE

Movie made in the USA in 1985
Poster: UK
Size: 30x40in (76x102cm)
Rarity rating: 3
Artist: Drew Struzan
Motor: De Lorean

196

CAR TROUBLE

Movie made in the UK in 1985 • Poster: UK • Size: 30x40in (76x102cm) • Rarity rating: 2 • Motor: Jaguar
Players: Julie Walters, Ian Charleson

Lovely rendition of the E-Type; if you look closely in the bottom right-hand corner, you'll see a little sketch of the Jaguar having its evil way with a Citroen 2CV. Should make for interesting offspring ...

CITY HEAT

Movie made in the USA in 1985
Poster: Italy
Size: 55x39in (140x99cm)
Rarity rating: 2
Artist: Napoli
Motor: Ford
Players: Burt Reynolds, Clint Eastwood, Madeline Kahn, Rip Torn

Rather stilted portraits of Reynolds and Eastwood, but a good one of the Model A

FERRIS BUELLER'S DAY OFF

Movie made in the USA in 1986
Poster: France
Size: 23x60in (58x152cm)
Rarity rating: 2
Motor: Ferrari
Players: Mathew Broderick, Alan Ruck, Mia Sara

This is the poster size that the French call 'pantalon'

FOXTRAP

Movie made in the USA in 1986
Poster: USA
Size: 27x41in (69x104cm)
Rarity rating: 3
Motor: Ferrari F1 car
Players: Fred Williamson

The music, the European scenery, and, of course, the poster were the class acts of this one

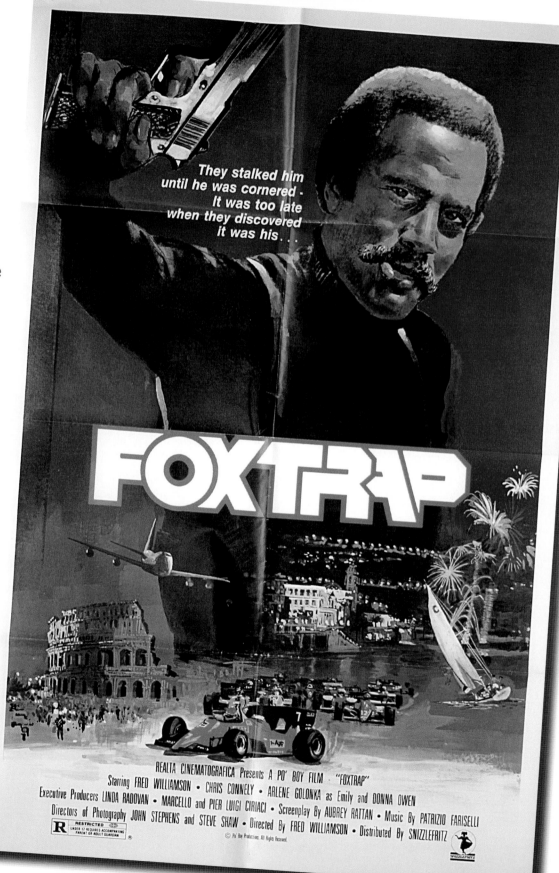

L'ENQUÈTE DE L'INSPECTEUR MORGAN

Movie made in the UK in 1986
Poster: France
Size: 60x23in (152x58cm)
Rarity rating: 2
Motor: Wolseley
Players: Joseph Losey, Hardy Kruger, Stanley Baker, Micheline Presle

This is a re-release poster of Joseph Losey's 1959 *Chance Meeting* (USA) or *Blind Date* (UK)

260 CHRONO

Movie made in the USA in 1987
Poster: France
Size: 47x63in (119x160cm)
Rarity rating: 2
Motor: Porsche 911
Players: D B Sweeney, Charlie Sheen, Lara Harris, Randy Quaid

Better known in the USA as *No Man's Land*

CHERRY 2000

Movie made in the USA in 1987
Poster: France
Size: 47x63in (119x160cm)
Rarity rating: 2
Artist: Casaro
Motor: Ford Mustang
Players: Harry Carey Jr,
Laurence Fishburne, Melanie
Griffith

Remember: the better the
poster, the worse the movie

LA RUMBA

Movie made in France in 1987
Poster: France
Size: 20x30in (51x76cm)
Rarity rating: 3
Artist: Goffaux
Motor: Delage – artist's impression
Players: Roger Hanin, Michel Piccoli, Niels Arestrup, Patachou

Very stylish Deco look

SLATE, WYN & ME

Movie made in Australia in 1987 • Poster: UK • Size: 30x40in (76x102cm) • Rarity rating: 3 • Motor: Cadillac
Players: Sigrid Thornton, Simon Burke, Martin Sacks

Set against the background of the Australian draft for the Vietnamese war, this was a beautifully made – but now largely forgotten – movie

THE LIVING DAYLIGHTS

Movie made in the UK in 1987
Poster: Japan
Size: 29x40in (74x102cm)
Rarity rating: 3
Artist: Brian Bysouth
Motor: Aston Martin
Players: Timothy Dalton, Maryam D'Abo, Jeroen Krabbe, Joe Don Baker, John Rhys-Davies, Art Malik, Desmond Llewelyn, Geoffrey Keen

Timothy Dalton is Bond; Maryam D'Abo is gorgeous

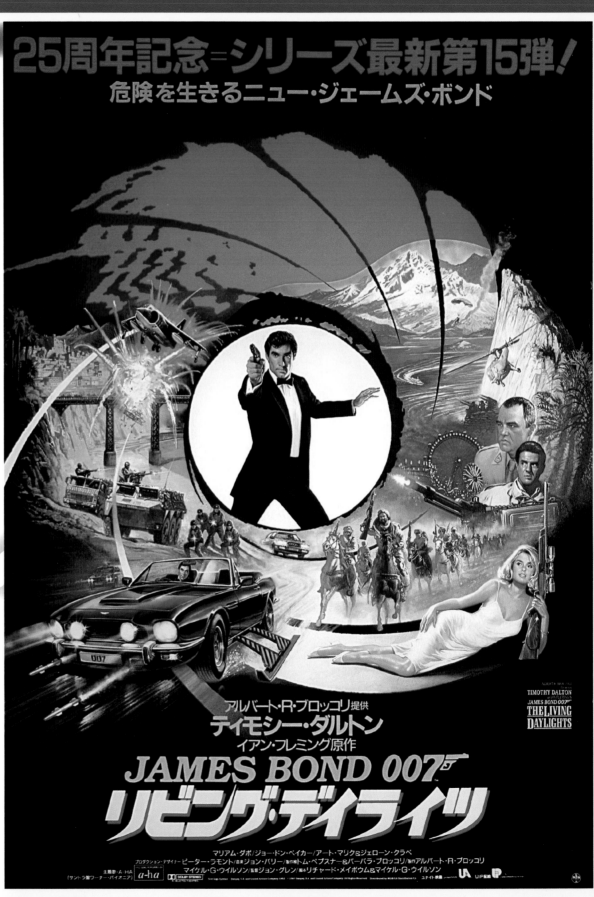

He built a car 20 years ahead of its time.
When Detroit tried to stop him he resisted.
When they tried to bully him he fought back.

When they tried to break him,
he became an American legend.

THE TRUE STORY OF PRESTON TUCKER.

A new film from George Lucas and Francis Ford Coppola.

JEFF BRIDGES

TUCKER
THE MAN AND HIS DREAM

LUCASFILM LTD. JEFF BRIDGES TUCKER THE MAN AND HIS DREAM JOAN ALLEN MARTIN LANDAU FREDERIC FORREST MAKO DEAN STOCKWELL JOE JACKSON DEAN TAVOULARIS VITTORIO STORARO (AIC) GEORGE LUCAS ARNOLD SCHULMAN DAVID SEIDLER FRED ROOS FRED FUCHS FRANCIS FORD COPPOLA UNITED INTERNATIONAL PICTURES RELEASE

Distributed by UNITED INTERNATIONAL PICTURES © 1988 U.I.P. ALL RIGHTS RESERVED

TUCKER: THE MAN AND HIS DREAM

Movie made in the USA in 1988 • Poster: UK • Size: 30x40in (76x102cm) • Rarity rating: 3
• Motor: Tucker • Players: Jeff Bridges, Francis Ford Coppola, Dean Stockwell, Mako,
Frederic Forrest, Joan Allen, Martin Landau, Christian Slater

Excellent portrait of Bridges as the heroic Preston Tucker, with a superb Art Deco backdrop

un uomo, una donna, e un coniglio creano un triangolo pieno di guai.

TOUCHSTONE PICTURES e STEVEN SPIELBERG presentano

Chi ha incastrato

ROGER RABBIT™

UN FILM DI ROBERT ZEMECKIS

AMBLIN ENTERTAINMENT

© 1988 Touchstone Pictures and Amblin Entertainment, Inc

TOUCHSTONE PICTURES

Distribuito dalla WARNER BROS ITALIA

WHO FRAMED ROGER RABBIT?

Movie made in the USA in 1988 • Poster: Italy • Size: 26x18in (66x46cm) • Rarity rating: 2
Motor: Benny the Cab • Players: Steven Spielberg , Bob Hoskins , Roger Rabbit

The Italian title appears to imply rather more dire consequences than we might have imagined ...

CATCH ME IF YOU CAN

Movie made in the USA in 1989 • Poster: UK • Size: 30x40in (76x102cm) • Rarity rating: 2 • Artist: Dewey
Motor: Chevrolet Camaro and Malibu • Players: Matt Lattanzi, Loryn Locklin

Dewey, the clever one, did the artwork. Huey and Louie, the not-so-clever ones, made the movie

HARLEM NIGHTS

Movie made in the USA in
1989
Poster: France
Size: 20x15in (51x38cm)
Rarity rating: 2
Artist: Drew Struzan
Motor: Packard – artist's
impression
Players: Eddie Murphy,
Richard Pryor

COUPE DE VILLE

Movie made in the USA in 1990
Poster: Italy
Size: 55x39in (140x99cm)
Rarity rating: 2
Artist: Anon
Motor: Cadillac
Players: Alan Arkin, John Considine, Patrick Dempsey, Arye Gross

The long-suffering Cadillac of this movie has been given a quite unwarranted vampiric appearance by its anonymous artist

STRADA BLUES

Movie made in France in 1990
Poster: France
Size: 20x15in (51x38cm)
Rarity rating: 3
Artist: Gelli
Motor: Mercedes-Benz
Players: Luigi Montini, Fabrizio Bentivoglio, Laura Morante, Diego Abatantuono

AKA *Turne*

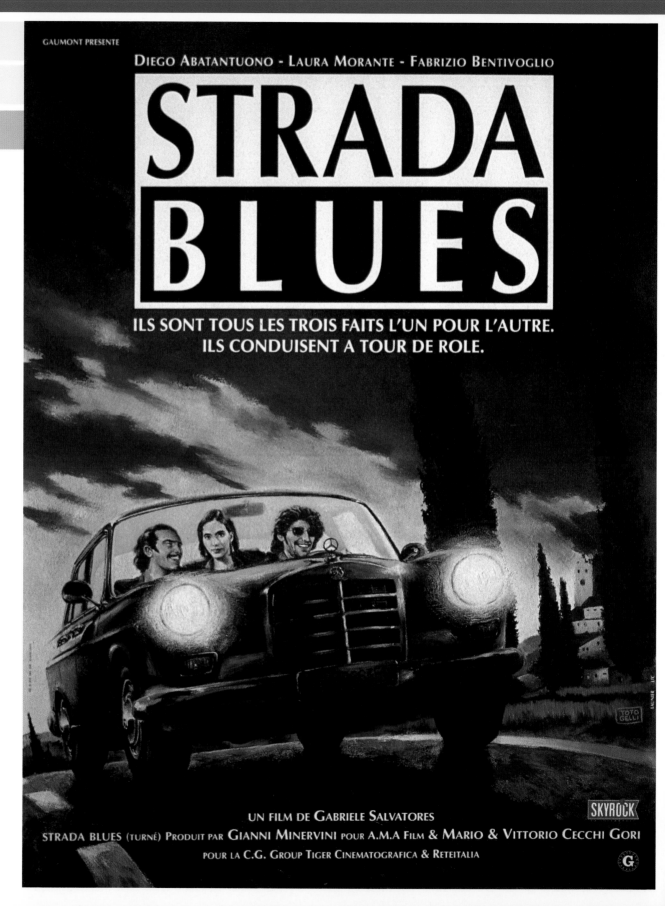

L'HOMME DE MA VIE

Movie made in France in 1992
Poster: France
Size: 47x63in (119x160cm)
Rarity rating: 3
Artist: Landi
Motor: Triumph TR3
Players: Maria de Medeiros, Thierry Fortineau

A pretty loose rendition of the TR3. Rather better of Maria de Medeiros

BLOOD, GUTS, BULLETS & OCTANE

Movie made in the USA in 1998
Poster: USA
Size: 27x39in (69x99cm)
Rarity rating: 3
Motor: Pontiac GTO
Players: Joe Carnahan, Dan Leis, Ken Rudulph, Dan Harlan

Cheerfully non-PC, low budget, all-action movie, with matching poster

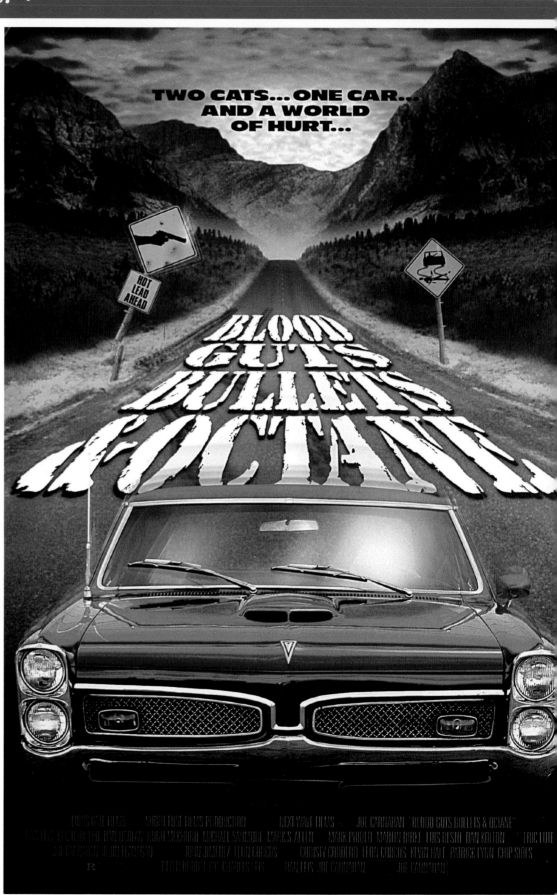

WHITE CAT, BLACK CAT

Movie made in Romania in 1998
Poster: Romania
Size: 27x38in (69x97cm)
Rarity rating: 2
Motor: Trabant
Players: Emir Kusturica

I'm unsure whether the pig is eating the Trabant, or deciding whether to move in. Either way it's probably a better use for the car than that which was originally intended …

OPERATION FANGIO

Movie made in Argentina in
1999
Poster: Spain
Size: 27x39in (69x99cm)
Rarity rating: 3
Motor: Maserati 450S
Players: Juan Manuel Fangio,
Dario Grandinetti, Hector
Alterio, Fernando Guillen

Great poster for a dire
re-telling of the Fangio
kidnapping, in Cuba in 1958

THE ITALIAN JOB

Movie made in the UK in 1969
Poster: UK
Size: 40x60in (102x152cm)
Rarity rating: 4
Motor: Mini-Cooper
Michael Caine, Noel Coward, Maggie Blye, Raf Vallone, Rossano Brazzi, Tony Beckley, Benny Hill, Irene Handl, John Le Mesurier, Fred Emney

The 30th Anniversary poster, which is more jingoistic, and places greater emphasis on the Minis than did the first release posters. This is the size of poster used on the ends of bus shelters in the UK, before the shelters were all vandalised

DRIVEN

Movie made in the USA in 2001
Poster: USA
Size: 27x41in (69x104cm)
Rarity rating: 1
Motor: Formula One 'Special'
Players: Sylvester Stallone, Burt Reynolds

Undoubtedly the best part of this movie is the poster

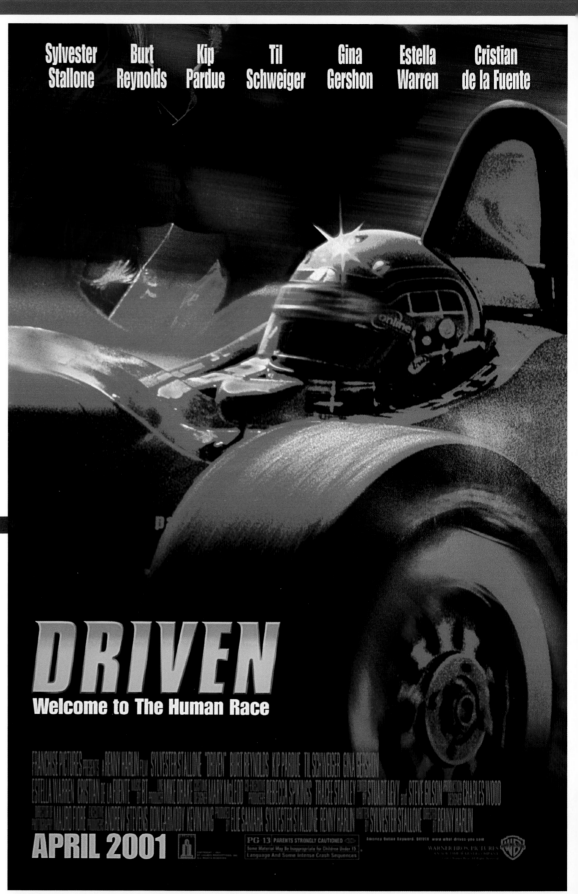

LAYER CAKE

Movie made in the UK in 2004 • Poster: UK • Size: 30x40in (76x102cm) • Rarity rating: 2 • Motor: Range Rover
Players: Daniel Craig, George Harris, Kenneth Cranham, Colm Meaney, Jamie Foreman, Sienna Miller, Michael Gambon, Dexter Fletcher, Tom Hardy

Daniel Craig getting a good kicking in preparation for being the new Bond

STARSKY & HUTCH

Movie made in the USA in 2005 • Poster: UK • Size: 30x40in (76x102cm) • Rarity rating: 3 • Motor: Ford Torino
Players: Ben Stiller, Owen Wilson, Snoop Dogg, Fred Williamson, Chris Penn, Carmen Electra

This is an 'advance' or 'teaser' poster, and in this case, has far better artwork than on the standard release poster

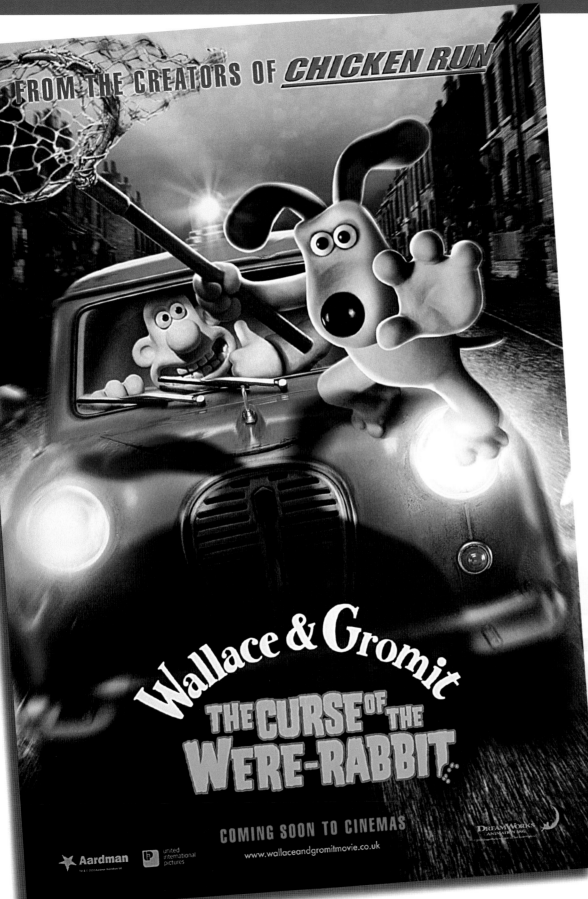

FROM THE CREATORS OF **CHICKEN RUN**

Wallace & Gromit

THE CURSE OF THE WERE-RABBIT

COMING SOON TO CINEMAS
www.wallaceandgromitmovie.co.uk

Aardman
united international pictures

DREAMWORKS
ANIMATION SKG

WALLACE & GROMIT: THE CURSE OF THE WERE-RABBIT

Movie made in the UK in 2005
Poster: USA
Size: 27x41in (69x104cm)
Rarity rating: 2
Motor: Austin A30
Players: Wallace, Gromit

Aardman's wonderful continuation of the life of Wallace and Gromit, brought to life in this poster

GLOSSARY

International variations in sizes and shapes of posters would take pages to explain, so I'll stick to the basics. Feel free to email me, or consult higher authorities if you need to know more. Recommended reference works are listed at the end.

In the USA the most common formats are the one sheet (27x41 inches/69x104cm), portrait), the insert (14x36 inches/36x92cm, portrait), and the half sheet (22x28 inches/56x71cm, landscape). There are bigger posters, referred to as three sheets, six sheets, etc, and smaller window cards and lobby cards.

In the UK the quad (30x40 inches/76x102cm, landscape) rules, with the one sheet (slightly smaller than the American version) supplied for the overseas market. Lobby cards in the UK are normally 10x8 inches/26x20cm, and come in sets of eight.

The two commonest sizes in France are the one panel (47x63 inches/120x160cm, portrait), and a smaller example measuring 23x30 inches/59x76cm.

Germany usually manages with two sizes: a one panel at 23x33 inches/59x84cm, and a two panel at 46x33 inches/108x84cm.

Italy has the locandina (13x28 inches/33x71cm, portrait), and its equivalent of the lobby card, the photobusta (26x18 inches/66x46cm, which can be portrait or landscape format. Size has varied over the years but it usually comes in sets of 6 to 12. Then there are the two sheet (39x55 inches/99x140cm), and the four sheet, or Quatrofoglio, printed in two sections and measuring, in total, 55x78 inches/140x198cm.

Japanese posters are usually found in four formats, although – as with other countries – there can be many variants. The chirashi, or flyer is 7x10 inches/18x25cm; the nakazuri, or publicity sheet, is 14x20 inches/36x51cm. The one panel (20x29 inches/51x74cm, portrait), and two panel (20x58 inches/51x147) seem to be the most collectable.

As you wander through *Motor Movies – The Posters!* remember that everything I have said is certainly right. Mostly. There are as many variations as there are certainties ...

I recommend the following publications if you want to know more:
• *Learn About Movie Posters* by Ed & Susan Poole (Guide Media of Chattanooga, TN, USA)
• *British Film Posters* by Sim Branaghan (The British Film Institute)

Other good sources are various works by Tony Nourmand, Bruce Hershenson, and Stanislas Choko. Of course, you can also visit www.drivepast.com or contact me direct, at paul@drivepast.com.

INDEX

STARSKY & HUTCH

HITTING THE STREETS MARCH 12